EIGHT-HOUR INVESTOR

EIGHT-HOUR INVESTOR

A Practical Guide to DIY Investing

Reduce Fees

Increase Returns

Take Control

CHAD TENNANT

Eight Hour Investor. Copyright © 2013, 2012 by Chad Tennant. All rights reserved.

Printed in the United States of America.
Cover and interior design by Chad Tennant

No part of this book may be used or reproduced in any manner whatsoever without the written permission except in cases of brief quotations (less than 300 words) embodied in critical articles and reviews. The scanning, uploading, and distribution of this book via the Internet or via any other means without the permission of the published is illegal and punishable by law. Please purchase only authorized electronic editions and do not participate in or encourage piracy of copyrightable materials. Your support of the author's right is appreciated and preserves the integrity of the book creation process.

For information about special discounts for bulk purchases, please contact us through www.8hrinvestor.com

The information in this book is for general reference and educational purposes only. This publication is not intended to provide tailored recommendations nor is it a basis for actions without careful analysis and due diligence. Investments are subject to risks and changes in values. The strategies in this book may not be suitable for every individual and the information is not a solicitation to buy or sell securities. This book is written primarily in the context of the USA and Canadian financial markets and contains data and analysis specific to. Neither the author nor the published are liable for any actions promoted or caused by the information presented in this book. Any views expressed herein are those of the author and do not represent the views of others.

Ironically a book that promotes indexing as a viable investment strategy has omitted a book index. This has been done purposely to encourage engagement with this book's material and content. All online links were operational at time of writing.

Find your voice, shout it from the rooftops, and keep doing it until the people that are looking for you find you."
— Dan Harmon

To those in pursuit of something greater.

What's one reason why you should consider do-it-yourself investing? The impact of fees!

Investment Approach	DIY Investor	Investment Advisor	Mutual Fund Salesperson
Initial value	$100,000	$100,000	$100,000
Years of growth	20	20	20
Rate of return	7%	7%	7%
Fees	.30%	1.30%	2.30%
Net rate	6.70%	5.70%	4.70%
Total	$365,837	$303,039	$250,572
Monthly time requirement	< 1 hour	1-2 hours	1-2 hours

Contents

I. The Big Picture — 5

II. Stand By Me — 21

III. First Base — 37

IV. Pizza Pie — 59

V. All That Glitters Isn't Gold — 73

VI. Everyone is Kung Fee Fighting — 93

VII. DIY Rises — 109

VIII. Let's Dance — 135

IX. Oh Canada! — 157

X. Fix You — 171

Introduction

Don't ask what your advisor can do for you; ask what you can do for your portfolio.

The top 20 percent of Americans hold 84 percent of the wealth, while the bottom 40 percent have just 0.3 percent. There is a good reason for this unequal distribution of wealth and it has to do with financial literacy and level of engagement. Those in the top 20 percent who made their riches, and didn't just inherit them, have one thing in common: a sound understanding of financial matters. Sure, other factors played a role in their success—passion, choices, relationships, and resources—but I reckon that to become wealthy is to be financially literate. Warren Buffet, Bill Gates, and Oprah Winfrey all have solid financial acumen; otherwise, they would be transferring wealth to others rather than receiving it. They would be squandering money as opposed to maximizing it. Conversely, 78 percent of former NFL players who go bankrupt within two years of retirement[1] had or have very poor money-management education.

Studies have found that many investors don't understand the most elementary financial concepts, such as compound interest and inflation.[2] Concepts such as these take an hour or so to learn, so what's the issue with learning them? Everyone gets 43,000-plus minutes each month to carry out various activities. A lot of those hours are allocated to work and quality time with family and friends. There is usually ample time left over for activities that can lead to increased financial literacy. However, people consume a steady diet of tuning in to "American Idol," "Dancing with the Stars," and "Judge Judy." Every Friday, Saturday, and Sunday, sporting arenas are full of passionate fans. Facebook, Twitter, and Call of Duty see plenty of activity. Walking the dog, going to the movies, and making regular trips to Starbucks also take up time, which leaves financial literacy off the priority radar. Don't get me wrong—I've enjoyed watching the Masters and Tweeting here and there, so I'm not suggesting that the aforementioned activities should be neglected; they bring us great joy. But why should financial literacy be neglected or be a low-level priority? Maybe people think they're getting a better return on time watching reruns of "Seinfeld" versus learning about investment strategy. The truth is that by keeping up with the Kardashians, people are falling behind on their financial prospects.

You might be thinking that you're better positioned than the rest. After all, you've hired an advisor who has you in a bunch of mutual funds or, better yet, has randomly selected some stocks and bonds. You're on your way to a secure and happy retirement, right? Wrong! Unless your advisor is completely conflict-free, objective, and transparent, your current investment approach will fail you in the long run. The majority of investment representatives are busy chasing sales targets. Portfolio managers are getting paid to gamble money while consistently under-performing the markets. Wall Street salaries and big bonuses depend on a food chain of television-watching, sports-obsessed Facebook investors to facilitate their existence. The best person to manage your money is you, and it starts with education. Isn't it a part of growing up to learn how money and investments work, along with being a steward of your own finances? Transferring thousands of dollars to advisors for their services is one option, but remind me again why you can't learn how to invest in three to six months. Perhaps you didn't learn about investing in high school or from your parents, but practical investment wisdom and information is highly accessible to those who seek it. It's a matter of getting engaged and being patient with the learning curve. It's a matter of finding balance and working before playing.

It's unlikely that anyone can do everything well by his or her lonesome. The more likely scenario is being a DIY where suitable while carefully hiring others to carry out specific duties. You should know what to look for when employing the services of others—for example, an insurance or real estate salesperson. Chapter Two provides tips for working with various advisors, consultants, and salespeople in any industry. If you're going to work with advisors, make sure you get the best results your money can buy.

Investors who employ investment advisors use them for the same reason they use microwaves: convenience. Whatever the reasons people hire advisors, the fact remains that many don't add superior value. Quite frankly, many of them are salespeople masquerading as diligent stewards of resources. Many investors readily embrace the client–advisor model without giving a second thought to managing their own money, which is to the detriment of their future prospects. Investors must wake up and smell the possible returns. That's not to say using an advisor is a bad choice, but making a choice from an informed position makes that choice much more credible. Ninety-nine percent of the time, the best person to manage your resources is you. Therefore, if after reading this book you decline the DIY investor path, make sure you hire an excellent investment steward.

The eight-hour investor is a type of investor who desires to manage his or her investments while committing the fewest amounts of hours doing so. Due to the proliferation of investment-friendly solutions such as target date funds, fund of funds, and exchange-traded funds, DIY investors are in a position to optimize portfolio efficiencies. DIY investors may choose to adopt a different or combination of other investor types as described in this book. Without knowing what the future has in store, no investor type is guaranteed success. It comes down to a few factors that will determine levels of engagement. Ultimately, when you undertake experiences and activities without desire, you almost always seem to come up short. DIY investing starts with becoming accountable for your own financial success and maintaining a desire to take control.

I wrote this book because I want investors to know that there are alternatives to the traditional client–advisor model. For those who are investment–savvy, they'll do fine, but for those with less savvy, it appears that sales rhetoric and complacency have gotten the better of them. The goal of this book is very straightforward: I want to help investors understand the various components of the financial landscape with a focus on Do-It-Yourself (DIY) investing. There isn't a lack of honest, helpful, and diligent financial professionals out there, but investing in particular is something investors can do for themselves while employing the services of specialists in other areas. The benefits of DIY investing are many and include reduced fees, increased returns, empowerment, knowledge, and independence.

To enter the ranks of the wealthy 20 percent is a difficult task that often calls for many sacrifices. Becoming a DIY investor, implementing smarter investment decisions, and improving financial outcomes don't call for much. In fact, becoming a diligent saver and DIY investor heightens the chances of becoming wealthy, or at the very least making the most of money invested. When you have completed this book and transformed yourself into a savvy investor, don't forget about impacting family, coworkers, and the community. Giving chocolate and movies as seasonal gifts is great, but consider the gift of financial literacy. If the 401(k) investment choices at work are compromised and inadequate, do something about it. If more needs to be done to ensure that small investors are on equal footing with large financial institutions, then make sure the government and Securities and Exchange Commission (SEC) mail boxes are full. Wall Street is not the enemy; the enemy is within investors who don't care enough about their money, lifestyle, and future. It's up to each of us to make the most of what we have.

I
The Big Picture

I'm not asking you to become a neurosurgeon.
I'm asking you to get involved in your financial matters.

Financial literacy is the bedrock of wealth creation, and the American foundation is weak. The lack of education produces a widening gap between the haves and have-nots. Individuals with poor financial acumen transfer wealth to others and "get by," while those with financial savvy attract wealth and amplify their lifestyle prospects. Money does not determine happiness, but options do, and options are fueled by money. The person who enjoys traveling, staying in fancy hotels, and dining can do so with financial resources. The person without resources who may enjoy the same cannot. Instead of self-educating with a plethora of free literacy resources available in libraries and online, the preferred literacy substitute and "new normal" now includes credit lines, credit cards, money advances, and teaser rates. So where exactly are Americans on financial literacy? A research report prepared by the SEC titled "Financial Literacy among Investors"[3] is quite telling. The purpose of the report is to assess the public's general financial knowledge. It includes excerpts from a report on the same topic conducted by the Library of Congress.[4] Here are a few of the highlights:

- Studies have found that many investors do not understand key financial concepts, such as diversification or the differences between stocks and bonds, and are not fully aware of investment costs and their impact on investment returns.

- Low levels of investor literacy have serious implications for the ability of broad segments of the population to retire comfortably, particularly in an age dominated by defined-contribution retirement plans.
- In a 2010 Northwestern Mutual Life Insurance study to determine Americans' general financial knowledge, 69 percent of the 1,664 participants failed the quiz. In the same study, only 32 percent of the participants could accurately define the term "index fund."
- In a 2009 Financial Industry Regulatory Authority (FINRA) study, only 21 percent of the respondents knew that bond prices typically fall when interest rates rise.
- Only 51 percent of participants in a recent online study understood how and when a financial intermediary receives compensation for sales of investment products in a hypothetical example. In the same study, 58.6 percent of online survey respondents incorrectly answered a question about calculating standard mutual-fund fees.

Financial Planning

Personal financial planning is the process of organizing financial activities to achieve lifestyle goals. It has a direct impact on an individual's standard of living and can have an impact on family, relatives, and other related parties while they are alive, and even after death. People have different interests, priorities, and goals, but at the root of our experiences is our financial standing. Think about it—what doesn't involve money or the transfer of value in some way? Our most basic needs consisting of food, water, and shelter requires money. It could be your money, a relative's, or the government's, but to exist means to afford. The foundation of planning begins with understanding the relationship among its components. Ultimately, planning and an understanding of it play an integral role in shaping personal experiences. It should be a top priority because it's highly correlated to experiential outcomes. For example, some people enjoy a better standard of living than others due to their financial and socioeconomic status. If we forgo an adequate amount of planning, we leave life events to chance and entertain a greater probability of financial hardship.

Many people are not taught basic financial management skills. Our educational system has let us down, causing poor financial literacy. A few people are taught by their parents directly or learn indirectly through adversity. Parents must realize that it's one of their primary duties to educate their children in preparation for a life based on finances. It's never too early to start learning about financial planning. In fact, conversations about the value of a dollar, opportunity costs, and saving for a rainy day are great lessons to teach children. By the time they reach their late teens and most certainly their mid-twenties, they'll appreciate and understand basic financial concepts. It's also never too late to start learning. Anyone can learn about financial matters by tapping into various sources such as books, blogs, television shows, and financial advisors. Many of these sources are highly accessible and affordable and often are very inexpensive—the Internet, for example. Better late than never because learning can help you change the way you manage finances and your behavior, leading to more fruitful experiences.

Financial planning is for everyone who comes into contact with money or resources of value. Even cultures that don't use currency in the form of coins and bank notes still require basic financial understanding to ensure that goods or services are exchanged fairly. Financial planning is an ongoing life activity because someone needs to manage bills, food, and shelter. Financial activities are simple for most teenagers, but they'll become more complex throughout different life stages and events. Compare those early career years, when the focus is debt reduction, with retirement years, when the focus shifts to income needs, estate planning, and providing for beneficiaries.

The planning process is a logical one by design and mirrors other processes used in different industries under difference names. For the most part, the process, shown below, is linear from the onset but becomes more flexible and iterative as time passes and things change.

Step 1: Obtain financial literacy and education.
Step 2: Outline goals, needs, and priorities.
Step 3: Gather, analyze, and consider relevant information.
Step 4: Develop strategies, plans, and ideas.
Step 5: Construct a financial plan with recommendations.
Step 6: Implement plan recommendations.
Step 7: Monitor the plan and make changes accordingly.

Financial-Planning Activities

Financial-planning activities can be divided into five broad areas: cash flow and money, risk and insurance, wealth accumulation and investing, and estate planning, with taxes affecting each. Figure 1.1 highlights the areas of financial planning.

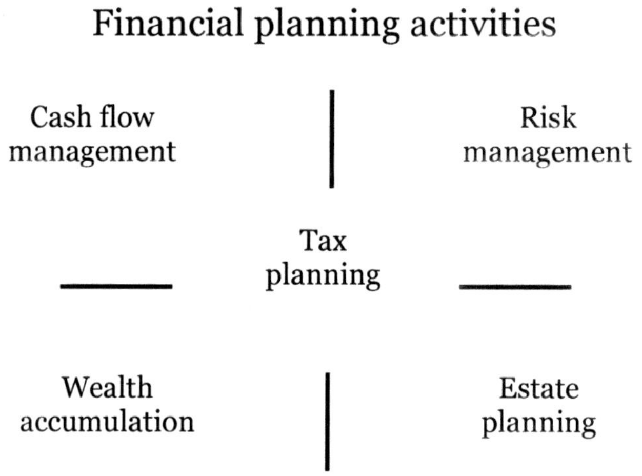

Financial planning activities

Cash flow management	Risk management
Tax planning	
Wealth accumulation	Estate planning

FIGURE 1.1. Financial-planning activities

Cash-Flow Management and Money

Cash-flow management focuses on the movement of money to support short- and long-term financial obligations. These activities cover activities like budgeting, spending, saving, and debt management. A *budget* is a document that itemizes estimated income and expenditures within a given time frame. Budgeting is more than a tool; it's a reflection of self-discipline and accountability. Responsible people, governments, and corporations all use budgets to understand their past, present, and projected inflows and outflows. Budgeting helps you gain short- and long-term financial perspective. Individuals' typical source of income is in the form of wages or compensation of some kind. Their expenses often include groceries, rent, phone, transportation, and clothing and extend to more personalized expenses such as skydiving, salsa lessons, and adventure travel.

A budget is essentially a forecast of upcoming income and expenses, but just as important are the actual inflows and outflows that should be used to calculate the final outcome. The actual numbers are what provide insight into cash-flow behavior. The common approach to budgeting is to use a specific time frame such as a month to capture activities. Starting at the top is the disposable-income section, which lists items such as wages, capital gains, dividends, interest, and other forms of income. The next section lists expenses such as groceries, rent, cable, Internet, and car payments. By subtracting expenses from income, the last section reveals a positive or negative number. If income exceeds expenses, cash flow for the time period is positive. If expenses exceed income, then cash flow is negative. As negative cash flows persists, this can lead to increasing levels of debt in the form of credit cards, payday loans, a line of credit (LOC), and other means used to substitute an income shortage. Figure 1.2 shows what a budget typically looks like.

April budget	
Income:	
Salary	$ 2,500.00
Dividends	100.00
Total Income	$ 2,600.00
Expenses:	
Rent	$ 1,000.00
Phone	50.00
Car	200.00
Food	200.00
Entertainment	100.00
Water/Electricity	175.00
Total Expenses	$ 1,725.00
Income − expenses	$ 875.00

FIGURE 1.2. A sample budget illustrating a positive monthly cash flow

Few people find budgeting exciting, and it may require missing a rerun of "90210," skipping a trip to Wal-Mart, and allowing the phone to ring. Yet it's at the core of all other financial planning facets. Budgeting isn't a complex activity, and its effort is dictated by the budgeter. Some people like to create a simple framework within which to operate, and others collect and record every detail. Financial circumstances and general money behavior influence the work required. In addition, technology, from software to mobile apps, has further simplified the budgeting process. Budgeting creates a sense of financial certainty and security that yields greater peace of mind. Understanding the flow of money into discretionary income allows you to spend, save, pay off debt, and/or invest after basic expenses are met. Similar to a plan or road map to climb Mt. Everest or complete a college degree, budgeting is a plan to get from one point to another. Finally, budgeting allows for review, change, and improvement of money-management activities.

Let's say your budget reveals a positive monthly cash flow of $400. You decide to spend $200 on a road trip and leave $200 in a savings account. *Savings* are composed of discretionary income not spent. Savings are a by-product of generating positive cash flow and, as such, are an indicator of money-management behavior. When you save, it provides allocation opportunities into other areas of planning such as insurance and investing. Savings differ from investing in these ways: Money isn't tied up, it's often exposed to little risk, and it attracts relatively low yields—for example, placing money in a bank savings account. It allows for the opportunity to accumulate reserves for one-off expenses like travel, home repairs, or unexpected emergencies. Savings also help you create peace of mind because you know financial resources are available if and when you need them. As a rule of thumb, maintaining savings equivalent to three, six, or more months of income is a good practice so that you will have cash reserves for an emergency or unexpected expense.

Debt results when you borrow money so that you have enough financial resources for a specific need. Debt management is geared toward activities involving creditors such as banks and credit card companies. A personal debt-management plan outlines how outstanding debt will be handled. For example, debtors may allocate a monthly fixed sum to reduce debt or apply as much as they can afford in an attempt to reduce debt more quickly. A mortgage is a common debt associated with home ownership, while student loans are commonplace among students.

Risk Management and Insurance

Risk management focuses on identifying scenarios that could be harmful to your financial and lifestyle status. This area of planning covers financial risks, lifestyle risks, and the products available to lessen the impact of those risks. A risk-management plan outlines strategies to protect against what-if scenarios should they occur. Because no one knows when they're going to die or become disabled or critically ill, insurance products transfer the risk of financial loss to another party in exchange for a premium. *Insurance* is a protection product designed to a hedge against a low-probability, high-probability, or untimely event. Private or personal insurance products are typically a contract between an insurance policyholder and an insurance company. The insurer promises to pay a beneficiary a sum of money triggered by a specific event. The premium paid is typically a fraction of the face-value coverage amount. Products are customizable from simple to complex, with additional benefits called *riders*. For example, a disability waiver of premium rider is intended to waive the insured's premiums if he or she were to become disabled.

Many of us have a standard of living we enjoy. Amenities such as the home we live in, the activities we share with our family and friends, the car we drive, and the clothes we wear make up our lifestyle. When a major life or health event occurs, it can have a devastating impact on our lifestyle, financial resources, physiology, and state of mind. Insurance isn't meant to solve all these related issues, but it can provide a degree of lifestyle and financial support if something happens. For example, on his way to work, John gets in a car accident and later is told by doctors that he won't be able to return to work for four months. As a result of his disability insurance, John will receive disability income payments while he recovers. If John did not have disability insurance, he would have to use his own financial resources to support himself during the recovery period.

Face-value coverage amounts differ from person to person and are a function of several factors, including affordability, goals, assets, liabilities, commitments, future needs, and lifestyle. Usually an insurance broker or agent will conduct an *insurance needs analysis* to determine the appropriate amount of insurance required. The insurance seller, typically an insurance company, determines an applicant's suitability based on several factors, including health, sex, age, type of insurance, face value, and family medical history. These factors are used in the underwriting review process by actuaries, specialists, and other stakeholders to approve or decline a policy application. Group insurance differs from personal insurance in terms of amount stipulations, transportability, eligibility, and other factors. The term "life insurance" tends to act as a catchall term, but there are, in fact, three main types of insurance products.

- *Life insurance* provides a payment to a beneficiary upon the death of the insured. There are various types of life insurance, ranging from coverage only to coverage with savings and/or investing features. *Term insurance* is the most basic type of insurance and, as a result, is more affordable than other types, all else being equal. The beneficiary may use the life insurance payout to stabilize his or her standard of living or to pay off outstanding debts, a college education, a funeral, and estate and afterlife expenses.
- *Disability insurance* provides a series of payments based on the insured's income if he or she is unable to work due to an injury or sickness. Disability coverage is divided into short- and long-term periods, with each period having its own set of stipulations. Many people have access to disability insurance through their employee benefit plans, but employees should review their insurance coverage to assess suitability.
- *Critical illness insurance* provides a payment after the diagnosis of a major illness, such as a heart attack, stroke, cancer, and many other illnesses. Similar to disability insurance in some respects, this type of insurance is considered a *living benefit*. Depending on the severity of the illness, the insurance payout may be used for home retrofitting, specialized treatment, medical equipment, mortgage protection, and career transition.

Once you have accumulated a fair amount of savings, you should commence insurance activities before or along with investment activities. The idea is to safeguard against the worst-case scenarios before focusing on the best-case scenarios. Insurance acts as a financial cushion to mitigate downside risks, whereas investments typically point toward a future need such as retirement. Without insurance, you may be forced to draw from savings or investments for financial support.

Wealth Management and Investing

Wealth management focuses on stockpiling financial resources for mid- to long-term needs. It covers topics such as investing, retirement, and pension plans. A wealth-management plan incorporates strategies used to accumulate, manage, and preserve money, primarily through investing. *Investing* is a wealth-building strategy that seeks to capitalize on a possession's increase in value. It's the commitment of money or capital toward something with the expectation of financial gain. Major investment categories include property (real estate), securities (stocks, bonds, or mutual funds), business ventures (start-up, franchise) and collectibles (stamps, art, or sports memorabilia). Accumulating enough financial resources is critical to fulfilling a desired lifestyle. Accumulating assets is a sensible endeavor because other income sources such as government benefit programs aren't enough to depend on as a sound financial plan. As it relates to securities, wealth accumulation focuses on maximizing each dollar invested while considering asset allocation, investment strategy, and fees. Investing should start after or along with insurance activities. Savings and insurance provide support for near-term and unexpected needs, whereas investing typically focuses on mid- to long-term needs.

When we contemplate our golden years and retirement lifestyle, many of us envision it without full-time work because we plan to live off our accumulated financial resources. Getting our resources where they need to be is a tough process because accumulation activities are thwarted by wealth-erosion factors such as inflation, expenses, and taxes. *Inflation* is the increase in prices of goods and services. Rising prices erode purchasing power because every dollar will buy a smaller percentage of a good at some point in the future. For example, if the annual inflation rate is 2 percent, then a $1 bus ticket will cost $1.02 next year. If you were to put a dollar under a pillow for a year earning nothing, that same dollar wouldn't be able to purchase the higher-priced bus ticket. If that same dollar earned 2 percent or more, it would have the same purchasing power as the year before.

Estate Planning

Estate planning focuses on afterlife financial matters and includes items such as estates, wills, and taxes. Estate planning is the process of anticipating and arranging for the disposal of an estate. It attempts to eliminate uncertainties over the administration of probate and seeks to maximize the value of an estate by reducing taxes and other expenses. *Probate* is the court process by which a will is proved valid or invalid. A *will* is the expression of how afterlife possession matters should be handled, and it's the preferred legal document regarding estate decisions. It directs the transfer of estate assets to beneficiaries. It also names executors or trustees to make decisions about estate assets.

Afterlife planning is just as important as planning while you're alive. This area of financial planning is often neglected, in part because it involves a very sensitive topic: death. It's also neglected because, to some people, estate planning is as interesting as budget preparation. However, both of these activities bookend the financial planning process and are vital to the creation, enjoyment, and transfer of wealth. Being proactive in afterlife planning can greatly reduce anxiety and stress for related parties. What if an unexpected fatal event were to happen a week from now? How prepared are you?

Estate planning is typically the last stage of planning because an estate usually is accumulated over a lifetime. Few twenty-year-olds have enough possessions to create a meaningful will; they are more likely focused on priorities like paying off student loans. Estate planning can be simple or complex depending on the stakeholders involved (family, friends, community, religious organizations, or charities). Other factors may involve business structures, investment accounts, or multiple properties.

Tax Planning

Taxes permeate all facets of financial planning, so it pays dividends to manage this area correctly. *Tax planning* is the process of aligning financial objectives with efficient strategies to minimize tax liability. Most people are familiar with filing their income tax documents, but tax law can become quite complex regarding the application of taxes to other sources of income. As it relates to securities, some investments are more tax-efficient than others because of the tax treatment they receive. An investment tax strategy focuses on aligning securities with the appropriate accounts to reduce the tax burden and considers the timing of buy/sell transactions.

The Basics

Becoming a DIY investor means understanding basic money and investment management concepts. How does someone accumulate riches? You can make and save more money. You can play the lottery in the hopes of hitting the jackpot or possibly bide your time for a future inheritance.

The above options are possible, but what if by making more, you end up spending more while saving less? What if, by winning the lottery, you are forced to share with other coworkers who copurchased the ticket, or the inheritance isn't the sum you had hoped it would be? Accumulating wealth doesn't have to be a task that deprives you or something that occurs by chance; rather, it happens by choice. You can choose to implement activities and principles on your way to accumulating riches.

A Penny Saved

Having money to invest comes from having positive cash flow. For example, let's say you earn $3,000, spend $2,000, and have $1,000 of discretionary income remaining. You can spend, save, or invest the remaining amount. Living for today would influence you not to save or invest at all. However, the popular 15 percent rule of thumb suggests that you should save 15 percent of your monthly gross income. Continuing with our example, the recommended amount to save would be $450 ($3,000 x 15 percent) a month. Conduct an online search for "how much should I save," and thousands of articles will appear about the 15 percent rule or similar recommendations. Perhaps to simplify things, a consensus was formed among financial experts once upon a time.

Either way, saving is more than a generic rule; it's a forward-thinking practice that doesn't stop at 15 percent. Let's face it, if the rule were 13 percent or 21.5 percent, people would be asking for some serious evidence to back up those claims. Fifteen percent, on the other hand, is a stress-free, achievable target, and it's easy to remember. Taking the forward-thinking practice of saving a step further, the road to wealth accumulation consists of ongoing decisions concerning money allocation. After taxes, every dollar earned has the potential to be spent, saved, or invested. People who consistently make wise decisions regarding the interplay of these options increase the likelihood of becoming financially successful over a lifetime.

The goal of saving is to put away as much as possible for the uncertain short- and near-term future. Saving impacts our life experiences as we balance money-allocation decisions between instant and future consumption. Basically, we can spend today or save for tomorrow. This relates to a concept know as *opportunity cost*, which is the cost of forgoing an alternative to pursue another. Let's say you are deciding between buying one of two cars with a budget of $30,000. Car A costs $30,000, and Car B costs $20,000. Buying Car A requires spending the entire budget, but Car A may offer greater enjoyment as it fulfills more qualitative needs like seat warmers and keyless entry. The financial benefit of buying Car B is having the ability to allocate $10,000 elsewhere (e.g., shopping, saving, and/or investing). The opportunity cost that hangs in the balance is the $10,000 that can be spent on a more luxurious car or be allocated elsewhere a number of ways.

The Compound Effect

Money increases in value due to the wealth-creation principle known as the compound effect. *Compounding* is the ongoing process of adding a new sum of money to an existing sum of money over and over again to attract even more money. For example, let's say you invest $1,000 in year one, and by year end, you receive a 7 percent return, for a total amount of $1,070. Starting in year two with $1,070, by year end a 7 percent return increases the amount to $1,144.90. The $70 gained in year one has attracted an additional $4.90 in year two. Compounding considers how many times money is compounded over and over to increase the initial value. Picture a snowball for a moment (even if it's 98 degrees outside). A large snowball doesn't usually appear out of thin air, and neither do millions of dollars in an account. By packing snow together to create a small ball and rolling it down a hill, it will eventually increase in mass and size to become a bigger ball. When rolling a snowball down a short hill compared to a taller hill, the taller hill will provide more opportunity for the snowball to increase in size. The hill height is representative of time, which is the compounding effect's best friend. The more time you have (the taller the hill), the more money can compound over and over. Less time means fewer opportunities to add layers of more money, thus producing a smaller sum. Time, frequency, and rate influence the future value of money. Figure 1.3 illustrates the impact of time based on a $10,000 investment that earns 5 percent per year.

Piles of money similar to a sequoia tree or the Empire State Building share one thing in common: They all started from something very small and increased in size over a period of time. The accumulation or future value of money is actually a very simple formula, but its discipline eludes many. As mentioned earlier regarding the practice of saving, the compounding effect takes place with something to compound on. It's surprising how much saving 15 percent per paycheck and allocating it wisely can appreciate over time.

Time and money

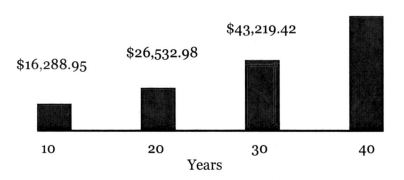

FIGURE 1.3. The result of $10,000 compounded at 5 percent annually

The Rule of 72

The Rule of 72 is a common and easy way to estimate how long it will take for an amount of money to double. It illustrates how a given rate of return or rates of return will impact the growth of money. For example, by dividing 72 by a 6 percent rate of return, an amount of money will double in twelve years. The term *basis point* is used frequently in financial circles as an alternative to stating a percentage for interest rates and return yields. Some people refer to 6 percent as "600 basis points." One percent is equivalent to 100 basis points. Therefore, 150 basis points would represent 1.50 percent.

So far, it sounds like it's pretty easy to accumulate money. Just save, let money compound, and focus on getting the highest rate of return so that money can grow. Not so fast! The Rule of 72 is convenient for doing quick math, but it doesn't cover the factors related to different rates of return. If comparing two rates— e.g., 6 percent vs. 12 percent,—a question should arise regarding the investment profiles associated with those rates. More to the point, what are the associated risks in pursing those rates of return?

Credit

Credit is the new wonder drug of financial activities and abides by the mantra "buy now, pay later." Need a new bike, television, or purse and don't have the cash flow? Just borrow the money by using a credit card or line of credit. Credit, like money, is neither good nor bad; it's the mismanagement of both that gets people into trouble. The 2008–09 credit crisis stemmed from masses of people gaining access to cheap credit through teaser and low interest rates. Many of these borrowers were poorly positioned in the first place and probably didn't consider budgets and debt-management plans, to their detriment. The planned use and payment of credit is OK, but when debt becomes insurmountable, it leads to financial, lifestyle, and emotional nausea. Using credit is about decision making. There are good uses for credit, such as education, home renovations, and investing, that seek to produce positive returns, and there are neutral to bad uses for credit, like consumer products and vices that don't seek to produce any monetary upside.

Here is how credit works. Let's say Bill has two friends, and both have asked to borrow money from him. Tom wants to buy a home stereo system for $1,000, while Doug wants to take a college course for the same amount. Bill loans them the money payable in one year at a 20 percent interest rate plus the return of the original amount. A year later, Tom pays Bill back the $1,200 for the use of his money, and Bill is overjoyed because he knows a 20 percent return is very difficult to get in the stock market. When asked about the stereo system, Tom remarks that the enjoyment lasted about six months. Doug pays back the $1,200 and tells Bill the course he took secured him a $5,000 salary increase at work.

The example above illustrates why companies like MasterCard and Visa are very profitable. Credit card companies dislike customers who pay off their balances in full and those who don't pay off their balances at all. However, they love customers who make their minimum monthly payments to keep the tab growing in perpetuity. This more than offsets the 1 to 3 percent of customers they've accounted for who won't payback anything. Charging customers 10, 20, and 30 percent like some department store chains is the norm. Payday loans are the bane of the credit industry and are normally situated in impoverished neighborhoods to take advantage of financially illiterate borrowers. Visit a wealthy suburb, and I guarantee there won't be any payday loan stores in sight. Borrowers should do their due diligence regarding the terms and mechanics of credit.

Eight-Hour Summary

Having a general understanding about financial matters goes a long way.

Despite the current status of financial literacy, optimism fills the air because the issue is being talked about much more than in the past. A solid financial plan helps people understand their current and potential future financial state. The process starts with understanding the planning framework. Many people hand this task to advisors, but they should be more engaged in decision making to influence their own outcomes. The remaining steps attempt to align goals, strategies, and activities to produce the most effective results. Cash flow, risk, wealth, and estate management are engulfed by tax planning. Each area of financial planning plays an important role in the overall picture. Not only are the areas interconnected to maximize and safeguard against possible scenarios, but effective planning helps make you all the more prosperous. To neglect financial-planning activities is to neglect a desired lifestyle. Getting a handle on the basics such as savings, compounding, the Rule of 72, and credit will improve your financial literacy, decision-making, and money-management skills immensely.

II
Stand By Me

Hopefully you have a great ability to discern between those who can help and those who can't.

The great thing about the financial-planning process is that there are people to help. Hiring advisors seems like the thing to do because many people don't really consider the DIY option. Although this book is about DIY investing, I'm not necessarily advocating DIY in every arena. Good advisors are useful, but lesser knowledgeable advisors who don't add value have the potential to reduce financial and lifestyle prospects. The value and expertise of top-notch advisors are always worth considering. Another consideration when thinking about hiring an advisor is how involved and complex your financial matters are. If very complex, it may be in your best interest to employ specialists. Think about the business owner or single parent who may already be juggling too many priorities. DIY financial activities on top of everything may add to the mix in a negative way. If you fall into the following four categories, using an advisor makes perfect sense.

DIY Exempt Categories

Category 1—Very Wealthy

This group's focus is on running corporations, doing philanthropy, and handling miscellaneous engagements. A lifestyle preoccupied with the very activities that created abundant wealth leaves little time to focus on financial planning. For example, the Richard Bransons of the world hire teams of advisors for their financial, business, and philanthropic affairs.

Category 2—Time-Deprived

This group of people consists of business owners, executives, single parents, and families with many children who don't have much spare time. For this group, using advisors while remaining engaged is a practical decision that lends itself to optimal outcomes.

Category 3—Living Comfortably

These people's financial resources far outweigh their desire to learn about financial planning. Maybe the person's not in the top 1 percent but lives comfortably and has no desire to learn about financial-planning topics. In this case, the person's priorities are elsewhere, and he or she may decide to employ professional services to handle personal financial matters.

Category 4—Can't Touch This

Some people just shouldn't touch money or go anywhere near it. Gambling, drugs, bad luck, or other negative experiences have impacted their ability to make sound financial decisions. Perhaps they have behavior and/or mismanagement issues, in which case an advisor overseeing activities is the best approach to optimizing financial activities.

The bulk of society doesn't fit into any of these four categories. Most people have the time to get more involved in their financial matters but instead misuse their time to focus on other, less important, priorities and activities. A balanced lifestyle includes many activities, and there is always room for taking ownership of your financial matters.

Credentials and Designations

Professional financial education, certifications, and designations are big business for government and for self-regulatory and academic organizations. The acronyms composed of three and four letters help distinguish as well as market advisory services. While there are only a handful of globally recognized designations and certifications, domestic educational bodies offer courses related to their country's financial framework. Financial curriculum has no secret sauce; there are plenty of books that reproduce the same information, but on a non-credit basis. Completed courses have no correlation to advisor execution; an advisor's success depends on his or her character, passion, engagement, and decision-making skills. Although courses provide knowledge, they are also used to track compliance of market participants and to reduce fraud. Most industry courses have basically four objectives:

- Help advisors gain industry access and employment.
- Serve as a point of reference for advisors' industry knowledge and education.
- Facilitate job-category compliance for specific careers, e.g., investment advising.
- Help advisors market their abilities, differentiate themselves from competitors, and gain knowledge.

The American College of Financial Services and the Financial Industry Regulatory Authority (FINRA) offer extensive lists of numerous designations at www.designationcheck.com and www.finra.org/Investors, respectively. Here is a short list of well-recognized financial designations. All other designations and certifications are usually subsets of these four:

- **Certified Financial Planner (CFP)**—Established by the Certified Financial Planning Board in 1969[5], the CFP certification is an integrated and comprehensive program that provides knowledge and strategies concerning all areas of financial planning. There are 140,000[6] members globally.
- **Chartered Financial Analyst (CFA)**—Established by the Chartered Financial Analyst Institute in 1962[7], the CFA designation is a graduate-level program that provides a strong foundation of real-world investment analysis and portfolio-management skills. There are 109,000[8] members globally.
- **Chartered Life Underwriter (CLU)**—Established by The American College in 1927[9], the CLU designation is an advanced-level program providing in-depth knowledge of insurance related to the needs of individuals, business owners, and professional clients.

There are 100,000[10] members globally.
- **Certified Public Accountant (CPA)**—Established by the American Institute of CPAs in 1887[11], the CPA designation is the benchmark for accounting and tax professionals. The program covers auditing, attestation, financial accounting, reporting, regulations, and the business tax environment. There are 386,000[12] members globally.

Advisor Listings

Financial advisors are here, there, and everywhere. The term *financial advisor* is a catchall for anyone who sells or services financial-related products. There are many different advisor positions within the planning framework. Financial advisors may be single, dual, or multidisciplined, combining the organic synergies among planning concepts. In some cases, passing an inexpensive course to become an advisor is all it takes, while other positions require significant coursework. Advisors who desire more knowledge and expertise always have the option of completing globally recognized and domiciled programs. The truth is, advisors are commodities themselves, but they are differentiated by the services they offer. Let's review who's available to help you, including planners, advisors, brokers, agents, lawyers, and others. Here is a list of common position titles and their descriptions:

Financial Planner

The term *financial planner* is often used interchangeably with financial advisor. However, three main activities differentiate these two positions:

- Financial planners create financial plans outlining clients' current and future financial status based on projections, financial resources, and wealth-erosion factors.
- Financial planners often have a broad understanding and application of the planning framework, including cash flow, risk, wealth, and estate and tax planning.
- Financial planners may or may not sell products, whereas financial advisors almost always do so.

Money Coaches

Money coaches are gaining popularity due to an increasing demand for professionals to assist people with budgeting, saving, and debt reduction, all of which fall under cash-flow-management activities. Some money coaches add a layer of behavior modification to help clients develop a healthy relationship with money, effective discipline regarding money, and a positive attitude toward money.

Private Bankers

Most people will usually come into contact with multiple bankers or tellers during their banking lifetime. However, a private banker, usually reserved for high-net-worth individuals, can help you manage cash-flow activities. Private bankers also may act as financial planners if their responsibilities extend to investment, tax, estate, and other activities.

Insurance Producers

Insurance producers sell life, disability, critical-illness insurance, annuities, segregated funds, and other insurance-related products. An insurance *agent* represents an insurance company by way of an agent–principal arrangement, which often limits product offerings. An insurance *broker* represents the insured and generally has no direct or few contractual agreements with insurance companies, allowing for more offerings and less conflict.

Investment Representatives

Investment representatives come with many different titles, but essentially there are two broad categories: *mutual-fund brokers* and *investment advisors*. The difference between the two types is their exam content, fees, licensing, compliance, and product offerings. Brokers are limited to selling mutual funds, whereas investment advisors can sell mutual funds, stocks, bonds, and exchange-traded funds (ETFs). An investment representative is responsible for selecting a mix of investments based on an investor's profile, which consists of personal details, goals, investment time horizon, and risk tolerance, among other details.

Investment Coaches

The field of investment coaching is a relatively new one that seeks to empower investors to manager their own money. The investment-coaching process brings together elements of teaching, coaching, and advising. A learning plan is followed to provide the client with the knowledge, resources, and tools to become a DIY investor. Investment coaches also may be licensed to sell investments, but generally speaking, they aren't seeking to sell products.

Portfolio Managers

Portfolio and investment managers are responsible for selecting investments based on a specific investment mandate. They focus on the day-to-day management of mutual funds, ETFs, hedge funds, or private equity funds. Although investment advisors may perform similar activities, the difference is in distribution, scope, and priorities. Investment advisors primarily focus on selling and client development, whereas portfolio managers focus on security analysis and deal with the fund's investors less frequently, if at all.

Tax Planners

Tax planners can serve the most basic tax needs, such as filing taxes or meeting more complex needs, such as those involving estate planning. Paying taxes is a certainty throughout life, and tax planners with an aptitude for financial planning can add tremendous insight into your financial situation. Tax planners can employ strategies regarding income, expenses, investments, life insurance, and estate planning to minimize taxes. They help business owners and individuals understand the intricacies of tax law.

Estate Planners

Estate planners tie together insurance, investment, legal, and tax activities to create financial plans that effectively dispose of estates. They may work in tandem with other advisors and are usually at the centerpiece connecting various stakeholders. Because this is the final piece of planning, estate planners have a heightened responsibility to fulfill client wishes.

Lawyers

Lawyers typically remain on the sidelines for the majority of planning activities. Their services often relate to estate planning, complex financial-planning scenarios, and divorce settlements. They also may form strategic business alliances to create what's known as a *family office*, which is a private company that provides, under one roof, all of the financial-planning services, along with miscellaneous services, usually to high-net-worth individuals.

Real Estate Representatives

Real estate representatives act as intermediaries between buyers and sellers of real estate property. Real estate representatives don't have a direct relationship to financial planning per se, but because real estate is the largest purchase many people make, the consequences have a significant impact on financial and lifestyle matters. Real estate economics should be factored into a comprehensive plan.

Mortgage Representatives

Mortgage brokers and *agents* arrange loans on behalf of individuals and financial institutions. Similar to real estate representatives, they don't have a direct relationship to financial planning. However, prevailing interest rates and mortgage terms significantly impact financial outcomes.

Eleven Qualities to Look For in an Advisor

While conducting an informal survey, I discovered that most people don't have a list of qualities they look for in an advisor. Many people engage advisors by way of convenience, chance, or referral by a family member or friend. Convenience occurs when an individual comes into contact with an advisor by walking into or calling a financial institution such as a bank, only to have a discussion that leads to a client–advisor engagement. Chance occurs when a relationship is formed by a random occurrence, such as meeting at a party. Successful advisors will generate many new clients by leveraging existing clients and getting referrals or introductions. There are major problems with these three ways of hiring an advisor. We're talking about planning for the future and getting it right once, not twice or twenty times. People should take great pleasure and due diligence in hunting for qualified advisors by developing a list of requirements. Some advisors have the salesmanship, but not necessarily the execution skills, so listen carefully to what they say during meetings. The following are qualities you should look for in an advisor:

1. Passion

People become advisors for many different reasons. Some become advisors because they've been promised a bunch of clients due to attrition, others are under pressure to follow in the family's footsteps, and some have the desire to make a lot of money. Asking a simple question like "Why did you get into advising?" or "What keeps you in this position?" can reveal a lot. Making the most of the advisor occupation means liking people and delivering a sound work ethic. Clients are at the very center of day-to-day operations, so an introvert probably wouldn't flourish in this occupation. Products and policies are always changing, so dynamic advisors who enjoy being up-to-date will yield better client results compared to those who resist keeping up with the ebb and flow.

2. Honesty

I hate to say it, but some advisors are dishonest, or at the very least dishonest with themselves. It could be of their choosing and may be influenced by a toxic sales environment. An honest day's work is one that is conflict-free so that the advisor can put the clients' needs far ahead of a paycheck. Unfortunately, clients are subject to advisor dishonesty and fraud as a by-product of poor financial literacy and a lack of common sense. A practical question to ask is "Where do I go to learn more about and/or to verify your credentials?" or "How do you tailor product offerings to different client profiles?"

3. Education

Informal and formal education both have there merits. Advisors who consistently enhance their knowledge and stay up-to-date with industry best practices are the advisors of choice. After all, "the mind is a terrible thing to waste," especially when it involves clients. Advisors should be doing more than fulfilling industry compliance requirements in the way of continuing education credits. Advisors working toward the completion of designations are demonstrating that they want to know more to be more. Advisors who stop at the basic entry-level requirements are usually focused on selling without a desire to optimize their clients' financial matters.

4. Experience

No amount of experience will lead to the perfect portfolio or tax plan because the financial industry is dynamic, not static. Advisors come and go, but a minimum amount of business tenure can indicate the likelihood of an advisor to stick around. Advisors who have been in business for less than two years are always subject to a subtle career change. The rigors of chasing and signing up new clients are why many individuals don't seek or remain in sales careers, especially those that involve earning commissions or fees. Many people don't want to take the risk of hiring advisors, only to have those advisors quit on them a few months later. A good measuring stick is someone who has stayed around for at least three to five years. Similarly, too much experience could mean advisor complacency or pending retirement, which could cause the advisor's abrupt exit out of the industry.

5. Target Market

Advisors who specialize in working with a particular clientele can gain proficiencies and equity in that market versus advisors who work with anyone and everyone. People have different profiles and various needs, so before selecting an advisor or being handed one, it's important to consider demographic profiling. For example, you may be a female who is looking for an advisor who works with women nearing retirement, or you may need an advisor who specializes in servicing young families. These specializations do make a difference in the client–advisor relationship.

6. Expertise

It's amazing how many advisors spread themselves thin in the hopes of appealing to everyone. I've met advisors who sell investments, insurance, and group products and find time to be branch managers, all in the same day. I mentioned earlier that advisors may be single, dual, or multi-disciplined, combining the organic synergies among planning components, but it's also important for your advisor to have a main area of expertise. By not doing so, advisors compromise their efforts and dilute their service offerings. For example, an advisor who focuses one-third of his efforts on investments, one-third on private insurance, and one-third on group insurance is not really a specialist in any of those areas. Although real estate representatives play an indirect role in financial planning, I would question the synergies and conflicts of a representative who doubles as an investment or insurance salesperson. A benchmark for advisor expertise should be a focus of 70 to 80 percent in one financial-planning area.

7. Product Offerings

Advisor product offerings should align with their specialties and target market. For example, an investment advisor who targets high-net-worth individuals should offer a full bag of investment products, not only mutual funds. When expertise, target market, and product offerings align, only then can the client's interest be served optimally and without compromise. Clients can get underserved and/or overcharged when those aspects misalign.

8. Freedom from Conflict

Is the advisor an agent or a broker? Why does the advisor select one product over the other? Does the advisor have any referral partnerships in place, and what is the financial arrangement? How does the advisor's investment strategy impact his or her compensation? These are just a few questions regarding conflicts of interest. Speaking with different advisors will help to spur additional questions. Ultimately, the desired advisor has adopted an independent and ethical framework and practices fiduciary duties that seek to benefit clients. Some credentials by default infer that those advisors follow a code of conduct, but some will and some won't.

9. Compensation Transparency

Advisors are salespeople and know that the elephant in the room is always the fee topic. People want advisors who are up front and who provide details of their business dealings such as licenses, business arrangements, privacy, client responsibilities, and above all, compensation.

It goes without saying that numerous client transactions get soured because of misunderstandings regarding fees. Advisors can earn income based on one or a combination of compensation models such as salary, commission, fee-based and/or fee only.

10. Stakeholder Focus

Advisors working with one another with clients as the focal point can be value-added. The responsibility of connecting stakeholders belongs to all those involved. However, you should seek out advisors who make this a common practice. If each advisor is working in isolation while focusing on the same client, it's very difficult to leverage different skill sets that may further optimize the client's financial dealings. I mentioned the family office concept of having several advisors under one roof. Indeed, family offices are geared toward high-net-worth individuals and families, but that's not to say others should be excluded. You can bind your advisors to form working relationships that create a synthetic family office arrangement. Advisors unwilling to work with others shouldn't be considered for hire.

11. Personal Traits

Personal advisor traits are those basic characteristics, such as expertise and success that make a salesperson exude confidence. Some advisors don't carefully consider these basic traits and, as a result, find little success when compared to the ultra-successful, seven-digit-income earners. Getting ahead is a matter of getting it right with the fundamentals of sales presence. Top advisors work to optimize the following characteristics:

- *Appearance:* An easy way to spot phonies is to assess the shininess of their shoes. An advisor's wardrobe speaks volumes. It projects a level of self-esteem and belief in his or her activities. Every piece of clothing doesn't have come from a major designer, but advisors should see their clothing as part of the sales process. Conversely, advisors who don't value their appearance or grooming could be less passionate and less interested in their activities than a more polished advisor.
- *Communication:* Outgoing advisors do more than just send random articles or birthday cards. Proficient advisors continually refine their communication activities and channel information to clients

that is relevant to them. They show a lot of initiative to keep in touch without going overboard, and they seek to have more than one meeting annually. What they discuss isn't just promotional; it's beneficial and educational to the client.
- *Consistency:* From day one, there is a consistent, sequential, and logical approach to their planning activities. Their methodology is solid but flexible, allowing them to embrace change and best practices. They understand the road map to success and present it easily.
- *Integrity:* Wall Street has often come under attack for showing the ugly side of business ethics. However, there are advisors who abide by high moral compasses with values permeating through their business model. While their business is rooted with client-enhancing principles, they make these principles part of their annual business evaluation.
- *Punctual*: Along with consistency, the best advisors have the discipline to arrive as planned. Expecting advisors to arrive on time 100 percent is unrealistic due to unforeseen circumstances like spontaneous road closures or unseasonable weather, but in such circumstances, these advisors attempt to notify clients of any delays.
- *Reliability:* The best advisors deliver superior service regularly, which equates to more than sales rhetoric and pie-in-the-sky promises. Clients quickly get a sense of these advisors who are on the ball and who follow up meetings with summaries of items discussed. They return phone calls and e-mails within twenty-four to forty-eight hours and provide sufficient details to reduce back-and-forth communication. You won't find these advisors playing "telephone/email tag."

Five Ways to Optimize the Client–Advisor Experience

Meetings

Client–advisor meetings can sure seem dull if one party is always talking. Engaging in active questioning and listening improves a client's financial education, awareness, and participation. Many advisors have it easy once clients decide to use their services. Instead of feeling empowered and getting engaged, advisor complacency sets in and the client's financial literacy stagnates. The line is very thin when comparing what many advisors actually do to what clients can do for themselves. Asking investment representatives generic questions about market conditions won't suffice. Questions such as those below help to make the most of meetings and client–advisor development. Consider asking your potential advisor these questions:

1. Are there any new products that would better suit my profile?
2. How are your services and/or business evolving to ensure greater financial security for me and my family?
3. Which courses are you taking at the moment and why?
4. How are my investments performing against their benchmarks?
5. Have you partnered with any other advisors or created any referral agreements since we last met? Would they benefit me?
6. Are there any financial-planning/investment books you can recommend?

Second Opinion

How many second opinions have I offered, only to hear "I'm well taken care of," which is the ultimate sin. I don't fault clients who have top-notch advisors, but top-notch advisors are few and far between. A second opinion could be as simple as a conversation with a prospective advisor. Similar to any other profession, financial advisors come in all sorts of "sizes," so the best fit is a worthwhile pursuit. Did you retrieve several opinions before you settled on your current roster of advisors? The financial industry demands that advisors take entrance courses and examinations, but advisors have interests and passions that help them excel in different areas. Some are stronger in investment selection, while others gravitate toward insurance planning. A second opinion concerning investments involves nothing more then providing some basic information, such as the current investment and asset mix. Some people think you need to disclose a lot of information, but in reality, a prospective advisor needs very little.

As for the second opinion, it should be based on objective metrics and not salesmanship. For example, an advisor should compare actively managed mutual funds to their benchmarks (stewardship), not to other actively managed funds (salesmanship). I don't suggest that you subject yourself to annual second opinions, but once every three years will refresh expectations and levels of service. The agenda should, at the very least, seek to validate performance, planning approach, fees, advisor capabilities, and product offerings.

Financial Education

Clients have a duty to learn about financial matters so that they can be actively engaged in influencing their outcomes. Improving the dialogue with an advisor, spouse, family, or friends creates a web of potential knowledge sources, and it helps keep the lines of communication open. Client education can come from various sources, such as newspapers, websites, blogs, magazines, seminars, television, podcasts, and social media. Selecting a favorable medium happens by trial and error. For example, you could focus on a different topic or topics for three months and then rotate to a different topic.

Advisor Connections

Elaborating on the "family office" concept, you should attempt to create a synthetic family office. By uniting advisors, you are empowering them to talk to one another to enhance planning activities. While each advisor learns more about the other, they'll work together to find a harmonious balance among financial areas to improve results for you.

Referral Reward

Advisors dream of having clients who spread the news of their services far and wide to others. Family, friends, and coworkers are then lured in by a client helping to build the advisor's client base and earning potential. Usually these client-referral magnets ask for nothing, but it's worthwhile do get something in return. I'm not suggesting that referring clients should become a full-time job, but should you bring in a client or two, why not claim something in return in excess of a thank you? A small token of appreciation from advisors in the form of a dinner, movie gift card, or charitable donation in your name may suffice. One of the toughest advisor activities is to find new clients, so having clients who are able to attract prospects is a very valuable resource. After a couple of successful advisor–prospect introductions, you should follow up with your advisor to establish an informal agreement if you feel there could be ongoing opportunities.

Eight-Hour Summary

Advisors are everywhere and available to service every need imaginable. Although our focus has been on financial advisors; life and business coaches, nutritionists, spiritual healers, and many others exist for various needs. In fact, we've become a society of advisors as a convenient way to offload many responsibilities that we could effectively manage on our own. Some folks are terrible with numbers or are more right-brained or have enough money to more than cover the cost of advisory services. Whatever the reasons, advisors should be used when is makes cost-effective sense to employ their services.

Competent advisors who demonstrate a commitment to learning through courses, workshops, and designations desire to apply new strategies that will benefit client endeavors. "Bird courses" and basic licensing requirements don't go far enough to ensure successful results from advisors.

Many of us are not taught how to select those we want to include in our business and relationship strata. However, there are traits that increase the chances of forming enduring mutually beneficial relationships. We looked at a few, but there are many more that can be brought into the fold. Finding and paying any advisor is easy, but evaluating and setting standards is worthwhile. Asking advisors for client references is a good way to determine how their current clients feel about them. Website testimonials could be outdated, but professional social media platforms may indicate how others view the advisor as indicated in recommendations and comments. Ask for references from clients who have been around for three years. Finally, whether you decide to do things on your own or hire assistance, the number one priority should be to maximize your efforts for a more promising outcome.

III
First Base

Hiring an advisor is a step toward investing, but learning about investments is the first step toward financial prosperity.

I find it amazing talking to investment representatives. They literally have a license to take people's money with the expectation of doing positive things with it. One would hope they have the know-how to make investment endeavors worthwhile for the many investors in client–advisor relationships. The sad truth is that some representatives are knowledgeable, while others are, well…not. Investment representatives should have an appreciation for various investment concepts that leads to informed decision making. The concepts in this chapter are concepts every investment representative should know, and if they don't, you have to wonder how committed they are to their profession and clients. Advised or not, investors flipping channels featuring financial news can easily get bombarded by terms and jargon if unprepared. It would be the same as going into a fitness class not having stretched or entering a brainstorming session without previous exposure to the topic. Investing isn't complicated, and it starts with understanding a few basics.

Asset Classes

An *asset class* is a group of securities that have similar characteristics, react similarly to market events, and are subject to the same regulations, laws, and governing bodies. The three traditional asset classes are cash (short-term products such as money-market securities), fixed income (bonds), and equities (stocks). There are also alternative asset classes like real estate investments and commodities (gold, silver, oil) that appeal to investors.

Cash

Cash can be considered non-invested money or money invested in short-term, low-risk, and highly liquid debt securities. Generally, short-term debt securities have commitment terms of ninety days or less—for example, Treasury bills (T-bills), promissory notes, and commercial paper. Cash in a portfolio may be in the process of being withdrawn or invested, or it may remain as part of an investment strategy.

Fixed-Income

With *fixed-income*, there's a promise to repay a principal amount borrowed on a maturity date while making interest payments in relation to the terms of a loan. In simple terms, a fixed-income security is an IOU from a corporation, government, or agency. For example, imagine your friend, Carole, is about to start a business. Carole has asked to borrow money from you. Her business idea seems viable, so you decide to loan her the money. In return, Carole will make interest payments with the full amount to be returned later. That's exactly how a bond functions. It is the most common security associated with fixed income.

Equity

Continuing with Carole's example, she's decided not to borrow money, but instead she offers a stake in her company by way of stock. One stock will represent a 1 percent ownership stake in her company. The price of one stock is valued at $100, so by giving her $1,000, you would own 10 percent of the company. The equity asset class commonly refers to stocks. A *stock* represents ownership in a corporation and a claim on part of the corporation's assets and earnings. Companies issue stock for the same reasons they issue bonds, which is to raise capital. Money raised could be used to fund various activities, such as a company takeover or new project initiative.

The lure of equities is that they have historically outperformed other asset classes such as cash, bonds, gold, and real estate over a period of decades. More importantly, equities have consistently outpaced inflation to protect from purchasing-power erosion. However, the rewards have come with greater volatility, with equities acting extremely turbulent during major bubbles and during world and economic events.

Real Estate

The most common approach to real estate investing is through purchasing a residential home. Commercial real estate, by contrast, can be very expensive to invest in. On the stock market, investors can access real-estate-based securities that facilitate exposure to residential and commercial activity.

Commodities

Silver, cocoa, sugar, and soybeans are commodities used in the production of other goods and services. As an asset class, commodities offer a range of choices for investors seeking diversification away from cash, bonds, and equities. Demand and supply factors, general economic conditions, and speculation all influence prices. A common approach to gaining exposure to commodities is through derivatives and managed products such as mutual, exchange-traded, or hedge funds.

Types of Securities

Bonds

Recall that a *bond* is basically an IOU, but officially a bond is a fixed-income security that is secured by a physical asset. This differs from a *debenture*, which is secured by something other than a physical asset, such as an issuer's credit rating. The terms often associated with a bond are its face or par value, coupon rate, price, yield, yield to maturity, and term to maturity. A bond's *face value* is the specified loan amount to be repaid at maturity. A *coupon rate* is the interest amount from a bond stated as a percentage. Similar to other investments, bonds trade at different prices based on supply and demand factors related to their characteristics, interest rate, and market conditions. They can trade at a discount or premium. A bond's *price* has an inverse relationship with interest rates. As interest rates increase, the price of a bond will likely move downward, and as interest rates decrease, the price of a bond will likely move upward, all things equal. A bond's *yield to maturity* represents the current payout rate stated as a percentage if the bond is held to maturity. The *term to maturity* is the time remaining before the face value is to be paid back in full.

Similar to stocks, bonds are traded between investors in a secondary market. A *secondary market* is used after an *initial public offering* (IPO) so that investors can buy and sell among each other, as opposed to the issuer. However, compared with stocks, bonds tend to be more diverse and less homogenous. As a result, most bonds are not traded in the secondary market through exchanges, but rather they trade *over the counter* or OTC. The OTC market consists of a network of *market makers*—companies and individuals who quote buy and sell prices for bonds, stocks, and other securities. Market makers provide liquidity by buying from sellers and vice versa from their own holdings, providing a seamless flow of transactions. An example of a bond offering is as follows: Company ABC is offering a ten-year bond set to mature December 1, 2023. The bond has a coupon rate of 3.50 percent per annum with interest paid semi-annually. The bond can be purchased in face value increments of $1,000.

Ratings

Similar to getting graded on a report in school, bonds are given grades to indicate their creditworthiness and quality. Independent rating companies such as Standard & Poor's (S&P), Moody's, and Fitch Ratings provide these evaluations based on an issuer's financial status and its ability to pay a bond's principal and interest in a timely fashion. Grades are assigned starting with A through D, and additional numbers, letters, and symbols are used to differentiate further. For example, Moody's may issue a grade of Aaa, Aa1, Aa2, and Aa3 to indicate a bond of high quality. Bond ratings change as a result of an issuer's financial status. An issuer's rating will have an impact on its offering because the rating will be compared to other available investment options. Bonds rated below BBB/Baa are considered speculative, non-investment grade and are also referred to as *high-yield* or *junk bonds*. Because the default risk is higher for junk bonds, issuers usually offer a coupon rate premium to compensate bond holders for the added risks.

There are various types of bonds, and some add marketable features such as convertibility, which allows for a bond to be converted into stock, for example. Bonds as an investment product are pretty straightforward because much is known in the disclosure of an issue. A bond's coupon rate, credit rating, and duration are factors that enable bond holders to project returns with some reliability. The primary objective with bonds is to collect a regular stream of interest payments, which differs from stocks, which are more prone to capital appreciation or depreciation. Investment-grade bonds are viewed as conservative investments, and in times of market turbulence, investors typically flock to bonds as a safer alternative to equities.

Stocks

The majority of financial news focuses on common stocks or "stocks." Common stock represents ownership in a company and entitles a shareholder to voting rights and dividends. Shareholders may be eligible to vote on a multitude of items concerning a company's affairs. For example, at annual meetings, shareholders are usually asked to vote for the board of directors.

A *dividend* is a payment issued from a corporation's earnings. Dividends are not guaranteed to be paid out or to increase, as some companies may decide to retain their earnings for other purposes. These companies believe that money kept within can be put to good use as opposed to giving it to shareholders. Factors that can affect payout are a company's financial status, dividend policy, and economic/market conditions. The issuance of a dividend is decided by a board of directors who meet periodically with management to review company reports and activities. Regular announcements are made in the press regarding dividend payout and increases, if applicable. A board can reduce or stop dividends. The attraction to common stock is the potential for capital appreciation and dividends. *Capital appreciation* is the increase in a stock's value, which occurs mainly due to positive company developments, events, and market conditions.

Consider two publicly traded companies, both in the technology sector. Company ABC produces a modern product that is fast, efficient, and user-friendly. Company XYZ produces a product based on older, less efficient technology that customers find difficult to use. We could refer to computers and typewriters or smartphones and mobile devices. Company ABC's sales and profit are growing at twice the rate of Company XYZ's sales and profit, and Company XYZ is experiencing decreasing sales and profit. Given these simple scenarios, it's easy to see which company investors would favor. Company ABC's product is leading to higher sales and profit, while Company XYZ's sales and profit are contracting. Without comparing Company ABC to another company, it's difficult to assess its prospects, but at the very least, it's operating in the right direction by increasing sales and profit. Investors buy or sell stock based on current fundamentals and future expectations. As demand increases for stock, investors seek to purchase that stock at the best available price. The opposite holds true for a decrease in demand as sellers seek to sell at the best available price.

Preferred stocks differ from common stocks in that they usually don't have voting rights, but they have a higher claim on the assets and earnings should a company declare bankruptcy. By default, dividends are paid to preferred shareholders before common shareholders. Preferred stock tends to act like a fixed-income security or bond because dividends are fixed and there is little potential for capital appreciation. In addition, many of the same factors used to construct a bond offering are used to construct a preferred stock offering. Like bonds, preferred stocks may offer convertibility to common stocks after a specified term.

Real Estate Investment Trusts

A *real estate investment trust*, or REIT, is a type of security that directly invests in residential and/or commercial properties. For example, a REIT may own shopping malls, office buildings, apartments, or retirement housing. An investor who buys a REIT is considered a unitholder and not a shareholder, and dividends are called *distributions*. These companies generate revenue primarily from rental income or interest collected from properties and then pass it on to unitholders.

Derivatives

A *derivative* is a security whose value is based on the price of an underlying asset, commodity, or other reference point. Underlying assets typically include stocks, bonds, commodities, currencies, interest rates, and market indexes. It's a contract between two or more parties that settles at a future date. One of the most important characteristics of derivatives is that the majority use leverage.

Leverage is the process of borrowing a sum of money based on an initial deposit or invested amount. For example, a derivative contract may be valued at $100,000 but may require only $2,000 to purchase. In this case, money is being borrowed at a ratio of 50 to 1 ($100,000 divided by $2,000). It's important to note that derivatives can be complex and should be well researched before you use them as an investment. Due to their use of leverage, gains and losses are magnified, and that can have a significant impact on your portfolio's performance.

Derivatives are used to hedge or reduce uncertainty, but investors also use derivatives to speculate to profit-from-market movements. The two most common types of derivatives are *futures* and *options*. A *futures contract* obligates a buyer to purchase an asset and a seller to sell an asset, such as a commodity at a predetermined future date and price. For example, a chocolate manufacturer goes long (buys) on a futures contract to secure a quantity and price of cocoa to reduce future price uncertainty. Meanwhile, a seller believes the price of cocoa will go down, so he goes short (sells) to secure a quantity and price to be sold at a future date.

An *option contract* provides the right, but not the obligation, to buy (*call option*) or sell (*put option*) a given asset, at a specified price (the strike price), during a period of time or future date. For example, rather than purchase a futures contract, the chocolate manufacturer would like to have the option to buy cocoa at a predetermined price, but should the price decrease, he will not act on the option. The chocolate manufacturer pays an amount known as a *premium* to have the "option" to go or not go ahead with fulfillment of the transaction. The premium amount is not refundable.

Managed Funds

A *fund* is a group of securities packaged together as one security for transaction purposes. It's essentially the difference between buying one peanut representing an individual stock or bond and a bag of peanuts representing many stocks or bonds. Managed funds are created by investment management companies that pool investor money for specific fund-investment mandates. For example, a fund's mandate may focus on purchasing US stocks. The majority of funds provide instant diversification by holding many securities, thus lowering the risk posed by holding just one security. Two investment strategies permeate the fund industry:

passive and active. *Passively* managed funds follow a predefined, transparent investment approach such as tracking an index, whereas *actively* managed funds are managed by portfolio managers who make ongoing investment decisions in an attempt to outperform an index or benchmark. The three most common types of funds are mutual, exchange-traded, and hedge funds.

Mutual Funds

Mutual funds are by far the most common and convenient investment choice for investors. Mutual funds come in two types: open-end and closed-end, but the majority of discussions involve open-end funds. Investment companies issuing open-end mutual funds continually issue (create) and buy back (redeem) shares for investors. Occasionally funds stop issuing new shares if total assets have become too large to carry out their stated investment objectives effectively. In contrast, a closed-end fund is a publicly traded investment fund that raises a fixed amount of capital through an initial public offering similar to a stock. The fund is then structured, listed, and traded like a stock or exchange-traded product on a stock exchange. Both open- and closed-end funds have a net asset value (NAV) that relates to a fund's price. A NAV is calculated by dividing the fund's assets (minus liabilities) by the number of shares outstanding. This is calculated at the end of every trading day by the investment management company. At the end of 2011, the Investment Company Institute reported the following details from its website: The global market for mutual funds sat at $23.8 trillion in assets, and with $11.6 trillion in assets, the US mutual-fund industry remained the largest in the world. There were 11,622 funds available to US investors, and of those, just 383 were passively managed funds with assets of $1.1 trillion.[13]

Exchange-Traded Funds (ETFs)

Although mutual funds still have a commanding lead in the managed fund category, *exchange-traded funds* have become a popular and advantageous alternative. ETFs are investment vehicles that combine key features of traditional mutual funds and individual stocks. Similar to mutual funds, ETFs represent a basket of securities that have an investment mandate. Like stocks, they can be bought or sold on exchanges, with their price available throughout the day (Open-end mutual fund prices are available at end of day). Most ETFs were designed to track market indexes—for example, the S&P 500. However, product innovation has expanded to actively managed, leveraged, inverse, and other types of investment strategies. In 2001, there were only 102 ETFs, but by year-end 2011, there were 1,134.[14] There has been significant growth in the United States and worldwide as investors clamor for these securities.

Hedge Funds

Hedge funds are investment vehicles that seek absolute returns in both rising and falling markets by using an array of investment strategies. Hedge funds are actively managed, employing various complex strategies such as buying, short-selling, spreads, arbitrage, and leverage. This differs from the majority of conventional mutual and exchange-traded funds that focus on buying and selling securities only. The term "hedge" used for hedge funds differs from conventional hedging, which seeks to reduce uncertainty.

For many decades, hedge funds were subject to minimal regulation compared to the disclosure requirements of other managed products. Only recently, due to the Dodd–Frank Act, hedge funds are required to disclose more information and to register with the SEC when funds total more than $150 million in assets under management.[15] Hedge funds often have high initial investment minimums ranging in the millions. They also tend to be illiquid because they typically require investors to keep their money locked in for a year or multiple years. Hedge-fund fees can vary but usually include two layers of fees: a base management fee, standard for managed products, of 1 to 4 percent and a second layer of performance fees. Performance fees supposedly act as an additional incentive for managers to generate profits. Performance fees can range from 10 to 50 percent of profits but normally call for 20 percent.[16] Without profits in a given year, only the management fee would be charged.

Private Equity Funds

Private equity involves raising money for and investing in privately held companies. While the IPO process allows the public to invest in companies transitioning from private to public, the majority of private equity comes from institutional and accredited investors who commit large sums of money for long periods of time.

Private equity funds invest in a portfolio of private companies. Private equity is raised for various reasons, such as to fuel growth and expansion, to take a company private, or to purchase a part of an existing company for conversion into an independent entity. For example, venture capitalism is a popular form of private equity in which start-ups seek money from venture capitalists to expand operations, as seen on the show "Shark Tank."

Fund of Funds (FoFs)

A *fund of funds* is exactly how it reads; it's a fund that invests in other funds, as opposed to a fund that invests in individual securities. The FoF approach is often referred to as a multi-manager investment approach. FoFs allow for broad diversification and can act as a one-stop shop for a particular asset allocation model such as balanced or aggressive. Similar to traditional funds, FoFs can be passively or actively managed while consisting of index or actively managed funds.

FoFs that are passively managed have assigned multiple fund weightings that are brought back into alignment as they drift. Actively managed FoFs execute what's called a "tactical" approach whereby the manager may over- or underweight certain funds, depending on market and economic conditions. In either case, FoF investors don't have to do any manual rebalancing. FoFs exist for mutual funds, exchange-traded funds, hedge funds, and private equity funds. Expense ratios are often higher than traditional funds because the underlying fund fees are added to the FoF fee. The associated fees can be found in a prospectus under "acquired fund fees and expenses" (AFFE).

Target-Date Funds (TDFs)

Target-date funds, or life-cycle funds as they are commonly known, have become popular investment choices for many investors. A TDF specifies a date/year in the future with the fund automatically adjusting its underlying asset mix from an aggressive to a conservative model throughout. For example, the Vanguard Target Retirement 2040 Fund is one of a series of life-cycle funds that uses a targeted maturity approach as a simplified way to meet investors' different objectives, time horizons, and changing risk tolerances.[17] The majority of TDFs use a FoF approach consisting of multiple funds. However, FoFs differ in that their investment objectives, and asset mixes are not dependent on a future date, nor are they expected to change from one asset allocation model to another.

Investment Risks

Risk, in the investment world, is the chance that an investment's actual return will be different (or less) than expected. This is measured by a statistical formula called *standard deviation*, but for simplicity's sake, it's the chance of actual returns deviating from expected return. Risk invites the chances of losing some if not all of an investment. However, keep in mind that risks come with the potential of upside rewards creating gains as opposed to losses. Given two investments with the exact same level of risk, all else equal, rational investors would select the investment that offers the higher potential return. Naturally, investors would want the best possible outcome for the least amount of risk taken. This is not often the case, so investors must decide to either take on less risk, which is associated with potentially lower returns, or more risk, which is associated with potentially higher returns. Of course there are never guarantees because the future is unknown and factors change. Figure 3.1 illustrates the risk–reward profiles of various securities.

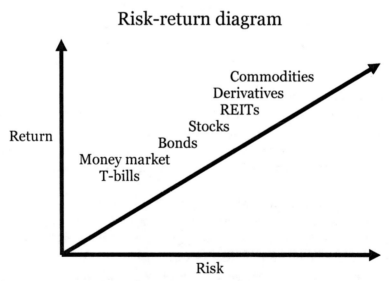

FIGURE 3.1. Risk-reward diagram

Risk has been inherent to investing since the beginning of time, and most risk can be managed in an effective manner. The concept of *diversification*, which we'll review in the next chapter, is basically the practice of placing many eggs in many baskets as a means to spread out risk among various asset classes and securities. By understanding risk–reward trade-offs, you can construct portfolios that address your aversions and appetite for risk based on several factors. Several risks are associated with investing; the level of their cause for concern depends on the asset class or security.

Default (or *credit*) *risk* is the risk that an issuer of a bond may be unable to make timely principal and interest payments. This can occur due to the poor handling of financial resources resulting in reduced cash flow and/or bankruptcy.

Business risk is the risk that a business will experience a sustained period of poor performance and earnings results amounting to lesser operational capabilities and/or bankruptcy. This can be the result of economic downturns, competition, poor innovation, ineffective management strategy, erroneous practices, and other internal and external factors.

Liquidity risk is the risk that a security cannot be traded (bought/sold) quickly and effectively enough in the market to make a profit, prevent a loss, or rebalance holdings. For example, a stock is halted by an exchange, rendering the stock untradeable. Liquidity risk is typically associated with securities that have low trading volumes, and, as a result, the difference between bid and ask prices is spread wide apart.

Foreign exchange (FOREX) risk is the risk that securities purchased using international currencies can be impacted positive or negatively by fluctuations in exchange rates. Many mutual and exchange-traded funds implement risk-management programs by hedging currency exposure to foreign currencies.

Interest rate risk primarily affects fixed-income securities and refers to the risk of changes in investment values as a result of movements in interest rates. This risk causes many market participants to follow comments made by the Federal Reserve Chairman (the Fed).

Market risk is the risk that security prices will fall due to factors that affect the market as a whole. A market may move downward for various reasons, such negative economic data and market sentiment, poor aggregate earnings, political instability, war, and natural disasters.

Inflation rate risk is the risk that prices in general (think consumer products) will outpace investment returns. For example, if the rate of inflation is 4 percent over the period of a year and the rate of investment return is 2 percent, then the investor has effectively fallen behind by 2 percent.

Investment strategy risk is the risk of using an investment strategy that underperforms the market. This could happen to investors who invest in actively managed funds that underperform their respective benchmarks.

Securities concentration risk is the risk that a portfolio's performance may be affected disproportionately by the poor performance of a few securities. If a portfolio tends to invest a high percentage of assets in only a few holdings, the performance of those holding will have a significant impact on returns. For example, a fund may hold sixty stocks, but the top five stocks may have a combined weighting of 60 percent.

Fund manager exit risk is the risk that a top-performing fund manager will leave a fund or fund company only to be replaced by a substandard manager. This can happen due to retirement, company reorganization, or acquisition.

Contango risk is the risk that a security or fund can deviate significantly from its underlying benchmark. Contango tends to be a niche risk relevant to commodity markets and commodity-type investments. For example, an ETF based on exposure to oil prices can deviate dramatically from increases and decreases in the price of oil.[18]

Investment Jargon

As an investor, you will navigate through the investment world, hear all sorts of terms, and be exposed to various products and topics. Some of these are used more frequently than others. Here are a few terms and concepts to help connect the dots even further:

Earnings Report

A quarterly or annual *earnings report* submitted by a publicly traded company shows its earnings, expenses, and net profit. These reports are also referred to as *income statements* or *profit and loss (P&L)* statements. Along with the earnings release, the media will indicate whether the corporation met, beat, or missed expectations. These expectations refer to a consensus by analysts regarding the projected results for that period. Many corporations arrange an earnings call, which typically follows an earning release. An *earnings call* is designed to enable corporate key stakeholders—e.g., the Chief Executive Officer (CEO) or the Chief Financial Officer (CFO)—to discuss the financial results of that period.

Earnings Season

Earnings season refers to the months of the year in which corporations announce and release their quarterly earning reports to the public. The four quarters are Q1, January to March; Q2, April to June; Q3, July to September; and Q4, October to December. January, April, July, and October are when earning seasons commence due to the timing and completion of accounting activities. It's not unusual for companies in the same industry or sector—banks or technology companies, for example—to report closely together.

Earnings per Share

Earnings per share (EPS) is the amount of reported income on a per-share basis. EPS is one of many ratios used to indicate a company's current status, future growth potential, and dividend payout, among other considerations. For example, let's say ABC Company has earned $13 billion over the past twelve months and has $10.5 billion shares outstanding. Therefore, ABC Company's EPS is $1.24 ($13B/$10.50B).

Price Earnings Ratio

The *price earnings ratio* or P/E ratio is the ratio between a company's current share price and its latest twelve month of earnings per share. Similar to EPS, the P/E ratio is a measure used for comparison against other stocks and historical averages. For example, let's say that over the past twelve months, ABC Company has earned $1.24 per share, and its current share price is $20. Therefore, ABC Company's P/E ratio is 16.13 ($20.00/$1.24). The term *multiple* is also used to highlight a company's P/E ratio. In the previous example, ABC Company is trading at a multiple of 16.13.

Dividend Yield

Dividend yield is a corporation's most recent full-year dividend per share divided by its current share price. For example, ABC Company pays an annual dividend of .68 cent per share, and its current share price is $20. ABC Company's dividend yield is 3.40 percent (.68/$20). Although ABC Company has earned $1.24 per share, by choosing to pay out .68 cent, this represents a *dividend payout ratio* of 55 percent (.68/$1.24). Dividend yields are used to compare against other yields of similar or dissimilar securities typically by investors seeking income.

Market Capitalization

Publicly traded companies are often differentiated by their size for investment-strategy purposes. Size is determined by a company's market capitalization or "market cap." *Market cap* is equal to the company's current share price multiplied by the number of shares outstanding. *Shares outstanding* refers to all the shares that have been corporately authorized, issued, and purchased. For example, ABC Company is trading at $60 and has 100 million shares outstanding for a total market cap of $6 billion. Size segments are divided into large, mid, and small cap.

Blue-Chip Company

A *blue-chip company* is a nationally recognized and well-established corporation that has demonstrated stability, consistency, and sound financial performance during economic cycles. Not all blue chips pay dividends, and those that don't may focus on stock buybacks and/or reinvesting profits to fund further expansion and growth. A *stock buyback* is when a corporation purchases its own outstanding stock for various reasons, but usually to raise the company's earnings per share. For example, XYZ Company earns $5 per share based on 100 shares outstanding ($5 x 100 = $500 in earnings). A buyback reduces the company's outstanding shares to 50, which, in turn, increases the earnings per share to $10 ($500/50 = $10).

Start-Up Company

In contrast to a blue-chip company, a *start-up company* is in the early stage of its development and typically faces a lot of uncertainty. It may operate at a loss for many years, and any profit made is likely to be reinvested to support further development and growth.

Market or Investor Sentiment

Market conditions are influenced by several factors, including current market values, domestic and global economic data, political events, seasonality, government, regulatory policy, and *market sentiment*, which is the general attitude of market participants. When market sentiment is positive, the markets tend to move upward, indicating strength, bullishness, and optimism. Negative market sentiment is when markets tend to move downward, indicating weakness, bearishness, and pessimism. For example, if the overall market sentiment is bullish or positive, stock values may increase with the expectation of better economic and corporate results ahead.

Initial Public Offerings (IPOs)

Private companies seeking to access public capital may choose to file an *initial public offering* or IPO. A company will usually hire an investment bank and other stakeholders for consultative duties regarding legal advice, marketing, share structure, and pricing assistance. The investment bank also will work in tandem with a securities commission to ensure that proper documents and financial statements are filed and approved. The IPO process can take up to several weeks of underwriting before the company gets listed on an exchange. Company information is disclosed in a prospectus, which includes financial statements, executive profiles, history, and other pertinent details so that investors can review details that were previously confidential. IPO news of popular privately held companies seeking publicly traded status can lead to a lot of hype, as was the case with Google, Facebook, and Visa. A cautionary note to investors is that an IPO is not a guarantor of success; in fact, many social media stocks that have recently come onto the market have performed poorly after their initial public offering and hype.

Stock Exchanges

Stocks commonly trade on *stock exchanges*, where buyers and sellers of securities meet to trade with one another after an IPO. There are two types of market platforms for buyers and sellers: a dealer market and an auction market. However, the two nuances of each platform essentially have zero impact and relevance to buyers and sellers. A dealer market uses *market makers* to execute trades and to provide liquidity to buyers and sellers. This is done over the counter or OTC on an exchange such as the National Association of Securities Dealers Automated Quotations (NASDAQ). Alternatively, the auction market allows individuals to buy and sell among one another, matching trades at the highest bidding and lowest selling prices. As opposed to market makers, *specialists* facilitate the matching of buy and sell orders. The New York Stock Exchange (NYSE) uses the auction market platform.

Indexes

An *index* is a group of stocks, bonds, or other securities used to track a particular market or sector. Indexes act as benchmarks and indicators of financial market activity. Indexes, in general, are constructed using predefined criteria for securities inclusion. For example, the S&P 500 Index includes the largest five hundred companies in the United States, whereas the Barclays (formerly Barclays Capital) Aggregate Bond Index tracks the total US investment grade bond market. As a benchmark, indexes are used to compare against the performance of other securities. Managed products such as mutual funds and their portfolio managers are constantly being evaluated against their underlying index benchmark. Indexes also serve as a reference point to indicate how financial markets are trending—i.e., upward, downward, or sideways. You will hear news reports that say, for example, that the Dow Jones Industrial Index is up 225 points.

The majority of equity indexes are *market cap-weighted*, meaning that stocks with the highest market capitalization will have the greatest weight and thus influence on values. The S&P 500, NASDAQ, and various global indexes are cap-weighted. Price-weighted indexes assign weightings by share price in proportion to the index's value. The Dow Jones Industrial and Japanese Nikkei are price-weighted. Other weighting methodologies include *equal weighting*, which assigns equal weight to all index constituents and *fundamental weighting*, which assigns weights based on fundamental factors such as sales, earnings, book value, cash flow, and dividends. For each weighting methodology, there are advocates and detractors. Popular equity index creators include Standard and Poor's (S&P), Dow Jones (DJ), Morgan Stanley Capital International (MSCI), and Russell Investments. Popular bond index providers include Barclays, Markit (iBoxx), and J.P. Morgan.

TABLE 3.1. Major US and world indexes

Major US and world indexes	Components	Country
Dow Jones Industrial	30 large-market cap (MC) stocks representing various industries	USA
S&P 500	Top 500 MC stocks traded on American exchanges	USA
NASDAQ	3,000+ stocks listed on the exchange and home of many large-cap technology stocks	USA
Nikkei 225	Top 225 MC stocks on the Tokyo Stock Exchange	Japan
DAX	Top 30 MC stocks on the German Frankfurt Exchange	Germany
CAC 40	Top 40 MC stocks on the Paris Bourse (stock exchange)	France
FTSE 100	Top 100 MC stocks traded on the London Stock Exchange	Britain
TSX Composite	Top 200+ MC stocks traded on the Toronto Stock Exchange	Canada
Hang Seng	Top 40+ MC stocks traded on the Hong Kong Exchange	Hong Kong
CSI 300	Top 300 MC stocks traded on the Shanghai and Shenzhen stock exchanges	China
Bovespa	Top 60+ MC stocks traded on the São Paulo Stock Exchange	Brazil
SENSEX	Top 30 MC stocks traded on the Bombay Stock Exchange	India

Bubbles & Crashes

A *bubble* as it relates to economics, securities, and real estate is a cycle of activity that leads to rapid expansion, growth, and significant increases in value. Conversely, a *crash* is a cycle of activity represented by a rapid contraction, reduction, and dramatic decrease in value. The dot-com crash is a good example. The popularity of Internet and technology companies around the turn of the century contributed to feverish demand for "new economy" stocks. Many investors wanted to buy into the promises and hoped that new technologies would bring dramatic changes, and many IPOs doubled in value during their first days of trading. It wasn't uncommon to see P/E ratios of 200, 300, and 400, with many companies having earned little or no profit, compared to historical P/E ratios of 15 for the S&P 500.[19] Along with their pie-in-the-sky business models, short operating histories, and lack of company vision, many of these companies reported huge losses after their IPOs. Investor enthusiasm quickly soured in Q1 of 2000, and the NASDAQ started its precipitous fall, losing 75 percent of its value as it fell from around 5,040 to under 1,120.

Gold

For thousands of years, *gold* has acted as a global currency, commodity, and investment. As a global currency, it was used as a medium of exchange among wealthy developed nations in the 1800s and late 1900s while used as a local currency in the form of coins. As a commodity, gold is highly malleable, ductile, and oxidation-resistant, making it useful in jewelry, dentistry, and industrial and electronic production. As an investment, there are periods when gold returns have outperformed other asset classes. Due to its low correlation to other asset classes, it's viewed as a good portfolio diversifier. As a hedge over the long term, through both inflationary and deflationary periods, gold has consistently maintained its purchasing power.

Oil

Crude oil and its by-products are the largest source of energy in the world. From gas-station fuel to power generation, crude oil is refined into many usable products that are integral to daily life. Known oil reserves are concentrated in the Middle East, which holds more than 50 percent of the world's reserves. OPEC, the Organization of the Petroleum Exporting Countries, is a group made up of mainly Middle Eastern countries that have the power to influence the price of oil by imposing supply quotas on member countries. Crude oil trades in barrels on different exchanges around the world but is often quoted in US currency—for example, $98 USD per barrel. The energy investment category can be very volatile due to supply and demand factors, political events, wars, and weather.

Investment Gurus

A nice way to round out this chapter is to mention a few investment gurus whose names regularly surface online, in discussions, and in books. When you consider how many portfolio managers have come and gone (tens of thousands) over several decades, it's amazing that only a handful stand out. To be an "investment guru" means to have achieved market-beating results worthy of mention. You don't make this group if you were a one-, three- or five-year wonder. Rather, discussions start after ten years, and that's only if you continue to perform under the spotlight.

Warren Buffet

Warren Buffet, 82, is the chairman and CEO of Berkshire Hathaway. As the poster boy for successful investing, he's often ranked amongst the wealthiest billionaires in the world, and he's has been the subject of many investment books. Berkshire Hathaway is a conglomerate that holds equity in many companies, some of which are household names such as IBM, Coca-Cola, P&G, Wal-Mart, and others. Buffet is well known for his outstanding track record of beating the S&P 500. From 1965 to 2011, the Berkshire stock returned 19.8 percent after tax, compared to a pre-tax return of 9.2 percent for the S&P 500. During that period, the overall gain for Berkshire was 513,055 percent, compared to 6,397 percent for the S&P.[20]

John Bogle

John C. Bogle, 77, is the founder of The Vanguard Group, which is the largest US fund company. He founded the Vanguard 500 Index Fund, the first index mutual fund, in 1975. He is a best-selling author, and *Fortune* magazine named him as one of the investment industry's four "Giants of the 20th Century" in 1999.[21] He has been an outspoken proponent of low-cost index investing.

George Soros

George Soros, 82, is the founder of the hedge-fund firm Soros Fund Management LLC. His private investment firm led to the creation of the Quantum fund. Soros is known as the man who broke the Bank of England due to currency trading that devalued the British pound and earned him a profit of around £1 billion. His Quantum fund average annual return was above 30 percent from the 1970s to 2000.[22]

Peter Lynch

Peter Lynch, 68, is a former portfolio manager of the Fidelity Magellan fund. He ran Magellan from 1977 until 1990, and by the time he stepped down, the fund had grown from around $20 million in assets to $19 billion, with more than one thousand stock holdings. Lynch's average annual return during those thirteen years was 29.2 percent, while underperforming the S&P 500 index only twice. He's considered one of the greatest mutual-fund managers in history.[23]

John Templeton

John Templeton, now deceased, was the co-founder of Templeton Funds, which was eventually sold to the Franklin Group (hence known as Franklin Templeton Investments). Templeton entered the mutual-fund industry in 1954, when he established the Templeton Growth Fund. With dividends reinvested, each $10,000 invested in the Templeton Growth Fund Class A at inception would have grown to $2 million by 1992. That represented an annualized average return of 14.5%.[24]

Eight-Hour Summary

Being able to differentiate among the various asset classes sets the stage for understanding the mechanics of investing. The three main categories are cash, fixed income, and equities, with real estate and commodities as alternatives. In lock step with these classes are their main representative securities, such as T-bills, bonds, and stocks, along with REITs and derivatives.

Managed funds are a convenient investment approach for many investors because they allow for efficient access to diversification through a portfolio of holdings. Investors have used managed funds for decades to create wealth with a plethora of innovations such as ETFs coming onto the market every day. Furthermore, fund of funds and target-date funds truly act as one-stop shops, requiring very little investment activity (hint: the Eight-Hour Investor method of choice).

Investments aren't without risks, but neither are other life experiences. Knowing risk considerations in advance can help you weigh the pros and cons, leading to a suitable investment portfolio.

The investment world has gone over-board with terms, concepts, and acronyms that do more damage than good. I have provided a few definitions in this chapter, and I encourage you to review those terms to improve your financial literacy.

IV
Pizza Pie

There is something for everyone, and it's just a matter of finding the sweet spot.

There is nothing like eating a great-tasting pizza, and if you feel the same, we're going to get along just fine. Pizza is one of the most diverse foods. Its open-minded base invites ingredients into a short-term marriage of fantastic flavor and color, yielding an exciting experience for the taste buds. Many Americans feel the same; they love pizza, as highlighted by a 2012 survey revealing that 97 percent of US adults eat pizza, and about 93 percent had gotten food from a pizza restaurant in the previous twelve months.[25] From pepperoni to Hawaiian to an exotic anchovy blend, what's not to like about a food that can appeal to the masses?

Like pizza, there are many layers to portfolio construction. The primary layer starts with looking deeper into asset classes. Similar to the array of pizza offerings, there is an equal number of possibilities available in portfolio arrangement. From a bird's-eye view, investors can be grouped into these various arrangements to suit their objectives and comfort. Conservative investors who may be rattled by stock-market news can find comfort in portfolios tilted to cash and fixed-income securities. For aggressive investors who can stomach dramatic market movements or high-volatility asset allocation, models are available for them. It's a matter of understanding the relationship between assets and how they have behaved historically in comparison to one another.

Asset Class Behavior

Asset classes historically have been uncorrelated. No matter what, fixed-income securities have behaved differently than equities over the long term and vice versa. Commodities and REITs also have behaved differently, as do any two asset classes you compare. There will be occasions when asset classes move in sync, but this tends to be an exception rather than the norm. To understand behavior among asset classes and securities, you must understand the concepts of *correlation coefficient* and *standard deviation*. Diversification is measured by a correlation coefficient, which determines the degree to which two variables move in sequence—e.g., two stocks. The correlation coefficient will vary from +1 to –1. A reading of plus one (+1) indicates that the variables are 100 percent correlated or related, whereas a reading of minus one (–1) indicates that the variables are 100 percent uncorrelated or unrelated. Table 4.1 highlights and describes correlation coefficient scenarios.

TABLE 4.1. Correlation coefficient scenarios

Correlation Coefficient	What will happen	Risk effect
+1.0	Variables will move exactly in the same direction.	Similar risks affect the two variables.
0	Variables will not move in sync.	Considerable risk reduction between two variables is possible.
–1.0	Variables will move in the opposite direction.	Risks between two variables are eliminated.

For greater insight regarding asset class behavior, we can study a couple of charts. The first chart, shown in Figure 4.1, illustrates the relationship between US stocks and bonds since the 1930s in five-year periods. The average correlation is just .20, indicating that the asset classes for the most part are neither 100 percent correlated nor uncorrelated, but somewhere in the middle, closer to zero. We can see that in 2005, US bonds experienced a correlation coefficient of approximately –0.6, indicating that bonds were likely to move "right" when stocks moved "left," whereas in 1975, with a reading close to +0.8, bonds and stocks where likely to move in lock step. In Figure 4.2, the chart compares different investment categories, which are subsets of asset classes, to how they've behaved compared to US stocks and bonds. We can see, for example, that international stocks from places such as Europe have traditionally moved in the same direction as US stocks, but US bonds and commodities are less correlated.

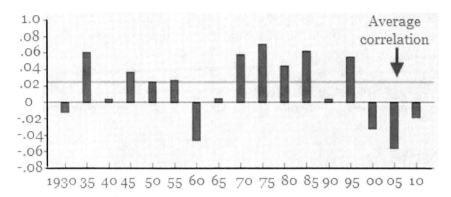

Source: Vanguard[26]
FIGURE 4.1. Five-year non-overlapping correlations between US stocks and US bonds

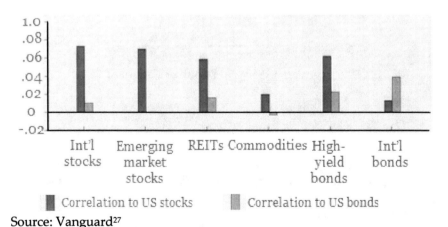

Source: Vanguard[27]
FIGURE 4.2. Monthly correlations between select investment categories and traditional asset classes: 1988–2011

Standard deviation, by contrast, indicates how much variation or movement occurs from the average of a variable. Equities have historically been more volatile (they have varied further from their average) than fixed income and cash. It's important to understand standard deviation to gain a realistic idea of how assets fluctuate in different market conditions. For example, investors who hold only equities in their portfolios can anticipate potentially large advances or declines during volatile market conditions. Although positive returns can be amplified during periods of significant volatility, some investors have a hard time coping with the opposite—e.g., a 30 percent drop in values, which can unfold in a matter of days or weeks under the same premise. So what does the volatility or range of movement look like for the three traditional asset classes? The following three figures provide a visual answer of activity over the last twenty-five years. Large swings represented by bars suggest that stocks can fluctuate significantly from their average, whereas bonds and cash experience only small to medium swings.

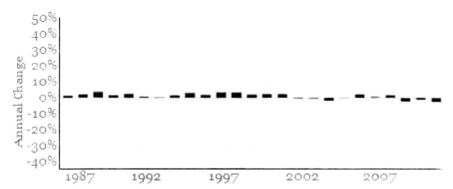
FIGURE 4.3. 100 percent cash 1987–2011 Source: Vanguard[28]

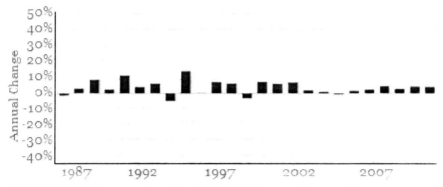
FIGURE 4.4. 100 percent bonds, 1987–2011 Source: Vanguard[29]

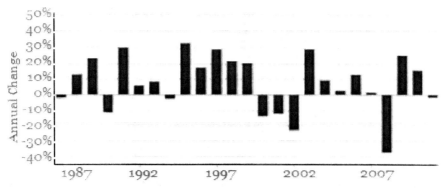

FIGURE 4.5. 100 percent stocks, 1987–2011 Source: Vanguard[30]

It's easy to see that stocks can range widely compared to bonds and cash. However, on the flip side, recall our discussion regarding risk and reward. The risk and volatility associated with stocks is much greater than with bonds, but so are the rewards. The table below illustrates the returns of each asset class given a full allocation over a twenty-five-year period. Also consider the Rule of 72 when reviewing Table 4.2.

TABLE 4.2. Performance results of US assets held from 1987–2011

	100% stocks	100% bonds	100% cash
Average annual return	7.76%	4.27%	1.09%
Largest gain in 1 year	33.07%	15.54%	3.82%
Largest loss in 1 year	-37.1%	-5.45%	-2.82%
# of years with a gain	17	21	18
# of years with a loss	8	4	7
$10,000 invested	$44,690.26	$27,727.94	$13,046.74

Source: Vanguard[31]

Asset Allocation

Asset allocation is the selection and assignment of financial resources among asset classes. It seeks to reduce risk by spreading resources among various investments. Deciding how to allocate resources is a by-product of understanding asset behavior and investor profiles in an effort to match them accordingly. Once upon a time, portfolio management was fairly basic, focusing on picking individual securities without accounting for their relationship to one another. In the 1950s, Modern Portfolio Theory (MPT) was developed by Harry Markowitz, who later earned a Nobel Prize for his work.[32] MPT basically states how a portfolio should be constructed to get the maximum expected return in combination with the least possible risk. Stated another way, it's how investors get the most bang for their buck without necessarily putting all of their eggs in one basket.

Two different bank stocks are likely to behave similarly in good and bad times. A bank stock and a military stock are less likely to behave in the same fashion and are thus less correlated. Central to MPT, diversification seeks to reduce the risk of holding similar securities by holding many unrelated securities. An additional consideration regarding diversification concerns those ill-fated stories of single stock ownership. Investors who don't consider diversification and own only one or a few stocks are subject to undue asset concentration risk. Consider Enron, WorldCom, Lehman Brothers, and others whose fortunes and shares prices collapsed dramatically within a short period of time. Also consider the 2008–09 financial crisis in which investors who tied their 401(k) accounts to a limited number of stocks and/or exclusively to equities may have experienced the worst of it. Diversification does have its limits, though, in line with the law of diminishing returns. Numerous studies show that diversification can be achieved by holding forty to sixty securities within an asset class, but as holdings are added, the additional benefit of diversification becomes less impactful. As a result, it's possible to carry the concept of diversification too far. A psychological drawback of diversification called *investor's remorse* occurs when investors wish they hadn't invested in certain securities. A portfolio review will indicate winners and losers, with most investors wishing that they had selected and diversified only to the winners.

Investor Profiles

An *investor profile* is basically the same as a pizza-preference profile. During the first or second meeting with an advisor, he or she will provide a ten- to sixteen-question risk profile questionnaire. Presto! In ten minutes, the advisor determines a client's profile to be "balanced" and invests half the money in fixed income and the other in equities. A few months later, the markets plummet and only then does the client realize that he's more conservative than the survey indicated. Losing sleep, the advisor frequently restates "the nature of the markets are to go up and down" or something similar to keep the client from leaving. However, this does little to calm the client's nerves. Deciding where and how to invest is more than a generic survey. It's an analysis that leads to a dynamic conclusion about how investors should be invested at a given point in time. There's a primary set of factors such as age, investment objectives, time horizon, risk tolerance, and knowledge that should be considered. Additional factors such as net worth, annual income, employment status, investable assets, and future investments add a second layer to the profile analysis.

Age

Age, as it relates to risk and time horizon, influences how assets should be allocated during life stages. For example, an investor in her late fifties who is close to retiring has a shorter investment time horizon compared to someone in his early thirties. All things equal, younger investors have years before they require retirement income and can ride out huge swings in market activity. Investors closer to retirement have less time to recover from large market declines and therefore may be better suited toward a more conservative portfolio (greater exposure to fixed income, lesser exposure to equities). Life-cycle investing provides allocation guidelines for different life stages.

Objectives

An *investment objective* is a desired outcome from investing activities. Common investment objectives include growth, income, and capital preservation. Investors focused on growth are building financial resources for milestones such as retirement, a major purchase, or a child's education.

Income-focused investors seek dividends and/or interest payments as a source of income. Investors who desire capital preservation seek to protect their principal from market downturns. These three categories are used as catchall buckets for specific goals such as those listed in Table 4.3.

TABLE 4.3. Investment objectives and specific goals

Objective	Specific goal
Growth	Building a retirement nest egg
Growth	Major purchases
Growth	Financial independence
Income	Retirement income
Income	Managing expenses or debts
Income	Charitable giving
Capital preservation	Preserving wealth for heirs
Capital preservation	Protection from disability or death
Capital preservation	Legacy donation

Time Horizon

Time horizon defines the amount of time during which money can be invested before it's required to make a transaction. The industry has conveniently created random horizon intervals such as one to three, three to seven, and seven-plus years. For example, an investor may have a three-year time horizon to purchase a car. Table 4.4 provides a general guideline of suitable asset classes for different time horizons in tandem with a completed investor profile.

TABLE 4.4. Time horizons and suitable investments

Time horizon (years)	Suitable investments
1-3	Cash and fixed income
3-7	Cash, fixed income, and equities (blue chips)
7+	Cash, fixed income, equities, and REITs
10+	Commodities, alternative and speculative securities

Risk Tolerance

Risk tolerance is the degree of volatility and declines an investor is willing to accept. Having reviewed how assets generally behave and standard deviation, some investors cannot stomach huge swings in portfolio values, while others are perfectly fine during bear markets and downturns. Unlike investment objectives or time horizon, tolerance also affects an investor's psychological and emotional state. Traditional classifications include low, medium, or high, as highlighted in Table 4.5.

TABLE 4.5. Levels of risk tolerance and suitable investments

Risk tolerance	Suitable investments
Low (conservative)	Cash and investment-grade fixed income
Medium (balanced)	Non-investment-grade fixed income and equities (large cap, blue chip, and value stocks)
High (growth)	All other equities, mid/small cap, emerging market, commodities and alternatives

Knowledge

Knowledge categorizes an investor's investment aptitude. Often overlooked by financial advisors, knowledge is extremely important in setting and managing expectations. However, investor knowledge can be difficult to assess without taking a standardized test.

Once you have a practical understanding of the above factors, you can make decisions about where to invest. Asset allocation is pretty straightforward, and the industry provides five main categories to help investors select an appropriate mix: very conservative, conservative, balanced, growth, and aggressive growth, with three models illustrated in Figure 4.6. Although these labels are widely accepted, the asset-allocation weightings are subject to variances from firm to firm, from advisor to advisor, and from investor to investor. Asset allocation weightings are very subjective because it boils down to personal preferences, usually within a range of 5 to 15 percent. For example, a balanced portfolio could represent a fixed-income to equity ratio of 60/40, 50/50, or 40/60, depending on the investment decision maker. Once you have chosen an asset-allocation model, the next set of decisions focuses on selecting investments within those classes. For example, the equity portion of a balanced portfolio could be divided into US, international, and emerging-market stocks. Additional layers can surface the more granular a portfolio becomes, so a third layer may seek to diversify among large-, mid-, and small-cap stocks. A forth layer may seek to diversify among styles, sectors, and other investment categories.

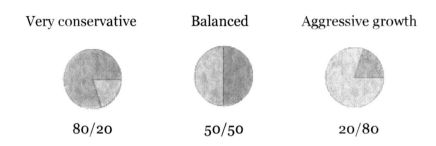

FIGURE 4.6. Asset allocation models

The Investor Life Cycle

Another way of looking at asset allocation is by considering the life stages of investors. The basic premise of life-cycle investing is that different age intervals attract different asset-allocation guidelines. Also called *age-based asset allocation,* the goal is to reduce exposure to volatility and market risk as investors approach retirement. This is the fundamental concept underlying target-date funds. Life stages are segmented into four intervals, starting in the mid-twenties and ending after the age of sixty. The intervals make assumptions about where people are in their financial journey and investor profiles. For example, an investor between the ages of twenty-five and thirty-four is starting to save while paying off school or mortgage loans, whereas an investor who is older than sixty is likely to be considering retirement options. As investors move through the life stages, the asset weightings change in accordance. Life-cycle investing also works with a general rule of thumb, which is that an investor's age should reflect the equivalent fixed-income weighting, give or take ten percentage points. Therefore, an investor who is forty-seven may have a fixed-income weighting of 37 to 57 percent to reflect her age. Tables 4.6 through 4.9 highlight investor life stages, but these are subject to interpretation, preferences, and personal circumstances.

TABLE 4.6. Ages 25–34 — Starting out

Objective	Saving and investing
Time horizon	Long term, 25 years+
Risk tolerance	High
Assets	Few
Debt	Post-secondary education, mortgage, and car loans
Allocation category	Growth

TABLE 4.7. Ages 35–44 — Investing diligently

Objective	Retirement savings
Time horizon	Long term, 15–25 years
Risk tolerance	Medium to high
Assets	Small to midsized portfolio, home equity
Debt	Post-secondary loan and mortgage
Allocation category	Growth

TABLE 4.8. Ages 45–59 — Planning retirement

Objective	Retirement savings
Time horizon	Medium term, 5–15 years
Risk tolerance	Low to medium
Assets	Mid-sized to large portfolio, home equity
Debt	Mortgage
Allocation category	Balanced

TABLE 4.9. Ages 60+ — Retirement living

Objective	Retirement income and capital preservation
Time horizon	Short term, <5 years
Risk tolerance	Low
Assets	Large portfolio, home equity
Debt	Debt-free
Allocation category	Conservative

Rebalancing

Rebalancing is the process of realigning portfolio weightings back to their asset-allocation targets. It involves buying and selling securities when weightings exceed predefined limits in accordance with the investor's profile. For example, let's say an investor has an original target allocation of 40 percent fixed income and 60 percent equities, or 40/60. Stocks have performed well over the last year, which has increased its weighting to 75 percent and reduced bonds to 25 percent. To revert to the original target allocation of 40/60, the investor would need to sell 15 percent of his equity holdings, then use the proceeds to purchase fixed-income securities, as summarized in Table 4.10. Many investors set deviation minimums of 10 to 15 percent so that they aren't continuously rebalancing. With generous leeway, investors can reduce trading fees and possibly tax consequences. It isn't always possible to rebalance to exact targets, though, so you should focus on making best efforts within one or two percentage points.

TABLE 4.10. Rebalancing example

Investor profile	Target asset allocation	Current	After rebalancing
Balanced	40% bonds 60% stocks	25% bonds 75% stocks	40% bonds 60% stocks

Eight-Hour Summary

Asset allocation isn't an exact science. It's an ongoing assessment that combines several variables such as an investor's age, goals, time horizon, risk tolerance, and knowledge. There isn't one perfect solution for everyone because investors have different profiles and seek different outcomes. Even if investors knew in advance that stocks would significantly outperform bonds in the near future, some investors would still be better suited toward a more conservative portfolio based on their investor profile. Although there are five allocation models, two need further discussion. If you favor being too conservative and decide to allocate 90 to 100 percent of your money to cash and/or fixed income, will your returns be sufficient to overcome wealth-erosion factors such as inflation, taxes, and fees? On the other hand, if you favor being too aggressive, with a 90 to 100 percent allocation to equities, are you willing to endure volatility without the safety and reliability of bonds? In both cases, you need to consider the rate of return required to fulfill your financial and lifestyle goals. As you learn more and monitor your portfolio, your correct allocation model will come into alignment.

For investors who are uncertain where to start, the asset-allocation topic will be explored further in future chapters. By default, new investors have the option to start conservatively and adjust weightings in tandem with their market experiences. For example, a DIY investor, age forty, could initiate a portfolio consisting of 50 percent cash and fixed income and 50 percent equities. In addition, it makes sense to commit to an asset model and investor profile for three to five years instead of changing annually. Frequent changes do not give a proper sense of profile alignment, and they potentially attract more fees generated by rebalancing activities. Life-cycle investment guidelines identify investment patterns for different age groups, but they don't truly reflect the "new normal" or societal changes such as people having to work past the average retirement age or children moving back home to live with their parents. Therefore, the guidelines and age parameters should be tailored to the individual investor's financial and lifestyle experiences.

V
All That Glitters Isn't Gold

Active management fuels an industry; passive management creates wealth.

I must confess, I was once on the active-management bandwagon, but then I saw the light. The licensing courses I had taken spoke little, if any, about passive management as a viable investment strategy. The poster boy for successful stock picking, Warren Buffet, acts as a beacon of hope and a constant reminder that beating the markets is achievable. However, only in hindsight can we appreciate the few who actually do so over a substantial period of time. I was challenged by investors (of the eight-hour sort) who laughed under their breath while I rang the Wall Street portfolio manager chimes. I decided to read outside the constructs of a biased industry. Lucky for me, I came across many good books, including *A Random Walk Down Wall Street* by Burton Malkiel. I was fascinated with his research and in-depth comparisons of investment matters. Only after reading his book and others of high quality can investors and advisors appreciate the song and dance of investment strategy.

Investment Strategy

An *investment strategy* is a method of security selection used to construct a portfolio for a desired result. Investment strategy may be directed by anyone, including DIY investors, advisors, and portfolio managers. Strategy choices fall into two main buckets: active or passive.

Active Management

Active management is a strategy whereby portfolio managers analyze and select securities with the goal of outperforming a market index or benchmark. Portfolio managers attempt to "beat the market" by using two main security selection approaches: fundamental or technical analysis.

Fundamental Analysis

Fundamental analysis is a process of analyzing financial statements to determine a security's "true" value and corresponding share price. Financial statements include balance sheets, income documents, and cash-flow documents, along with comments made by a company's management and board of directors. Analysis of documents leads to forecasts that paint a picture of what a stock is currently and possibly worth in the near future. Fundamental analysis also takes a look at the fundamentals of the marketplace, competition, and economic environment. Once an estimated true value has been determined, the fundamentalist would buy the security if it's underpriced compared to that value. If the security is overpriced compared to the estimated value, the fundamentalist would not invest and would perhaps sell (or short-sell) the security.

Analysis of XYZ Company

Thomas is interested in buying XYZ Company. He is a strong believer in doing his homework regarding investment analysis, with the goal of understanding a company's future prospects. He starts by examining five years worth of XYZ Company financial statements and notices that the company has increased profit by 10 percent each year. XYZ Company has very little debt, and it has increased its dividend every year for the past five years by 20 percent. Today, XYZ Company is trading at fifteen times its earnings at a share price of $45. Similar companies are trading at twenty times their earnings. Thomas believes the company will increase earnings and dividends next year, which will justify a higher price-to-earnings ratio. In addition, he believes the company will trade at a future multiple closer to its peers, so he decides to buy XYZ Company.

The above is a simplistic example of fundamental analysis activities. Wall Street analysts undergo much more rigorous fact-finding and valuation techniques because their decisions involve billions of dollars. Analysts focus on several key quantitative and qualitative metrics, such as a company's P/E ratio, debt-to-equity ratio, profit margin, dividend payout, EPS, sales penetration, market share, innovation, and the strength of management.

Technical Analysis

Technical analysis is the process of analyzing historical market information in an effort to forecast probable future price trends. Market information includes three primary sources: price, volume, and time. Unlike fundamental analysis, which seeks a security's true value, "technicians" and "chartists" evaluate charts and other quantitative indicators to identify possible future price patterns. Technical analysis is based on the following three assumptions:

- *The price reflects all known information.* Technicians believe that fundamentals and economic data are built into the price, eliminating the need to do further analysis.
- *Prices move in trends, and those trends tend to persist for relatively long periods of time.* According to Newton's laws of motion, an object continues in motion unless compelled to change by external forces acted upon it. Technicians apply the same logic to market trends and their direction.
- *The future repeats the past.* Technicians believe that patterns and trends are likely to repeat themselves. Studying the past helps you identify possible future buying and selling opportunities.

A common place to start in technical analysis is by drawing lines that indicate support and resistance levels, creating the appearance of a channel. In Figure 5.1, the Whole Foods chart indicates bullishness and upward-trending prices starting from early 2010[33]. The support line on the bottom illustrates the price level at which demand is considered to be strong enough to prevent the price from declining further. The resistance line on the top illustrates the price level at which there is selling pressure to prevent the price from increasing further. Technicians will apply various chart formations and statistical indicators in tandem with price and volume to confirm buy or sell opportunities. Popular chart formations include Head and Shoulders Top, Rising Wedge, Flag, and Cup with Handle. Popular statistical indicators include Moving Averages, Relative Strength Index, and Bollinger Bands.

FIGURE 5.1. Support and resistance lines Source: Stockcharts.com

Passive Management

Passive management (also called passive or index investing) is an investment strategy that seeks to replicate the holdings of market indexes. Investors can think of it as "buying the market" without the use of rigorous forecasting, market timing, or security-selection techniques. It relies on buying baskets of securities from different asset classes and investment categories. For example, an investor decides to invest in equities (asset class) by selecting the Russell 2000 Small Cap Index fund (investment category). Theoretically speaking, it's impossible to buy the Dow Jones or S&P 500 indexes, but index funds, mutual funds, or exchange-traded funds seek to represent their holdings and aim to replicate their performance and movements (minus a low management fee). For example, the Vanguard S&P 500 ETF (VOO) invests in stocks held in the S&P 500 Index. Generally speaking, passive management as a strategy is less costly than active management. Index funds generally have relatively low turnover, yielding lower transaction costs. Index funds are less likely to be tied to advisor compensation, whereas compensation-tied, actively managed funds are commonplace. Third, index funds don't attract the high compensation costs associated with active-investment management activities and market research. Actively managed funds can have high overhead caused by employment of managers and analysts to assist with research.

Hybrid Investing

Hybrid investing (or custom investing) is somewhat of a new kid on the block, combining a mix of passive-management and active strategies. Active strategies differ from active management in that active strategies consist of predefined transparent security selection and allocation guidelines. Active-management strategies are confidential and known only to those associated with the portfolio or fund. It's important to note that hybrid indexes are not traditional market indexes and, as such, are not intended to be a measurement or indicator of anything. They are investment strategies designed by their creators for various investment objectives. For example, an S&P 500 hybrid fund includes those securities that meet predefined criteria such as having increased sales, increased dividends, and increased profits for each of the past five years. Hybrid investing techniques have gained popularity in association with the growing demand for ETFs.

Fund Styles

There are different styles of investing as it relates to security selection. Investment managers may focus on investing in value and/or growth stocks. They also may focus on investing in high- or low-quality bonds. *Value stocks* tend to trade at low multiples relative to their fundamentals and can be unpopular with investors. By "unpopular," I mean that these stocks don't receive as much media attention and have low analyst followership. Value stocks are characterized by high-dividend yields and low P/E ratios. It's important to note that these stocks may be "cheap" for very good reasons, such as deteriorating market share, lack of product innovation, poor execution, and mismanagement. Conversely, *growth stocks* tend to trade at high multiples relative to their fundamentals. They can be all the rage with investors—for example, social media stocks such as Facebook, LinkedIn, and Groupon. Growth stocks trade at high P/E ratios because earnings are expected to grow at above-average rates compared to the general market. It's not uncommon to come across growth stocks that have P/E ratios above 100.

Morningstar, an independent investment research company, introduced the Style Box[34] to help investors understand fund investment styles, as illustrated in Figure 5.2. The equity grid classifies securities by market cap and style. The fixed-income equivalent classifies securities by investment grade and duration.[35]

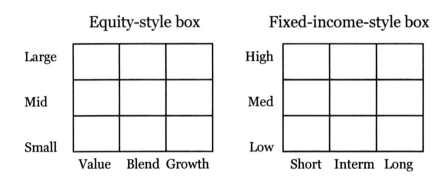

FIGURE 5.2. Equity and fixed-income style boxes

The emergence of ETFs has spawned new fund-style dimensions. First-generation ETFs were fairly straightforward because many of them focused on replicating popular indexes. As second-generation ETFs surfaced, they became slightly more complex and confusing to some investors. Some of these second-generation ETFs are hybrid funds because they reference established indexes and then apply active strategies. To help investors understand ETF investment styles, Richard Ferri[36] pioneered an index-strategy-style box incorporating different types of investment strategies and weighting methodologies, as illustrated in Figure 5.3.

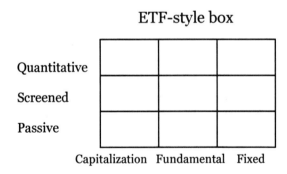

FIGURE 5.3. ETF index-strategy-style box

Security Selection

The left side of the ETF index-strategy-style box represents three investment strategies: passive, screened, and quantitative.

Passive selection is the equivalent of passive management, whereby securities held match those of market indexes and benchmarks.

Screened selection is equivalent to hybrid management. It filters through a broad list of securities and excludes unwanted securities that don't meet predefined criteria. Criteria may be based on fundamentals, philosophy, or any range of miscellaneous factors.

- *Fundamental investing* involves selecting securities based on fundamental factors such as cash flow, sales, and dividend payout. The thought here is that criteria-matching securities will outperform other securities that don't measure up.

- *Philosophical investing* is based on selecting securities that comply with specific values, beliefs, or activities. Some of the considerations include business ethics, religion, green practices, and product message. For example, a fund that consists of "ethical" securities would exclude companies that profit from alcohol, cigarettes, and gambling activities. Although performance remains a top priority for investors who select philosophically based investments, these same investors are equally concerned about a company's business status and practices.

Quantitative selection is somewhat equivalent to active management and depends heavily on computer usage and modeling to find securities that offer potentially superior rewards.

Security Weighting

The base of the ETF index-strategy-style box represents three different weighting strategies: market cap, fundamental, and equal weight.

Market cap weighting is associated with passive management. As investors dictate market cap values, securities receive weightings relative to other securities. In market-cap-weighted funds, high-value securities dictate performance; big value swings in those securities can impact results significantly.

Fundamental weighting assigns weights to securities based on fundamental criteria. The criteria could be based on financial ratios such as the P/E ratio, technical indicators, or philosophical compliance. Securities with the highest fundamental scores are assigned higher weightings.

Equal or *fixed* weighting assigns an equal or fixed percent to securities. By assigning equal weight, smaller market-cap securities become as impactful to overall results as larger market-cap securities. Equal weighting seeks to mitigate asset concentration risk by reducing the impact a few securities can have on performance.

Active vs. Passive Debate

A few decades ago, passive management was viewed as an insane approach to investing. John Bogle, founder of the Vanguard Group, introduced the first index mutual in 1975 to an unreceptive industry audience. After all, portfolio managers were backed by designations, valuation models, analysts, and technology to outperform market indexes. With all of those tools and insights, surely active management would prevail—or so we were to believe. Fast-forward to current times, and actively managed investments still dominate the asset landscape. Despite irrefutable evidence and results that support passive-management strategies, index mutual funds attract less than 10 percent of total US mutual-funds assets.[37]

Who consistently outperforms the market? The market is made up of thousands upon thousands of investment professionals the world over. That's right—there are professionals in London, Mumbai, Tokyo, Toronto, and Sydney, and many of them are trying to beat the market. A market's value is determined by professional and unprofessional participants, with professionals having greater influence. In the professional category, we have portfolio managers, chief investment officers (CIOs), market makers, designated brokers, professional traders, institutional investors, analysts, advisors, and many other financially savvy individuals. In the unprofessional category, we have retail investors, day traders, and gamblers.

Concerning most retail investors in the advised client channel, the responsibility of outperforming the market rests on the shoulders of portfolio managers. It would be nice to think that each portfolio manager is dramatically different than the next—for example, Bob employing an investment strategy from Neptune, Janet from Venus, and John from a galaxy far, far away. The reality is that most professionals drink from the same Kool-Aid, and they are more similar than different.

They're looking at the same stocks and data as their neighbor. They're employing similar tactics of securities valuation and selection, which leads to *strategy neutralization*. When investors consider how many professionals and to what extent their collective efforts contribute to a market's value, the chances of one or a few individuals outsmarting millions seems ludicrous. This, however, hasn't stopped the industry from promoting and celebrating the few portfolio managers who do beat the market in an effort to feed wishful thinking. The investment gurus mentioned in this book are few are far between, which is why they are celebrated in the first place.

Active Manager Selection

Is there a sound approach to selecting future outperformers? The short answer is no, and the long answer should be borrowed from the short answer. Investment management companies love to advertise past results. No matter the duration of success—e.g., one, three, or five years—or how small the incremental gain, active-management marketing stops at no end. Companies do this to imply that future results can be linked to the past while adding a small print disclaimer that reads "Past results aren't indicative of future results."

Common sense tells us that betting on a baseball player to replicate his four-home-run performance in the following game would not be wise. Yet thousands of investors rush to invest in the star portfolio manager of the day, usually through their advisor, in the hopes of continued success. More often than not, when star portfolio managers are identified, money inflows exceed their ability to manage allocations effectively. Investors hate to see money sitting in cash, so portfolio managers are forced to invest, given the increased spotlight, whereas before, they operated with more flexibility. In *A Random Walk Down Wall Street*, Malkiel compares how the top twenty equity funds performed in one decade versus the next. Tables 5.1 through 5.3 highlight decade-to-decade performance results. Malkiel also cites an article in *The Wall Street Journal* that mentioned how fourteen mutual funds had beaten the S&P for nine consecutive years through 2007, but only one continued that feat in 2008.[38] Selecting managers based on past results has no correlation to future success.

TABLE 5.1. How the top twenty equity funds of the 1970s performed during the 1980s

	Average annual returns	
	1970s	1980s
Top 20 funds of the 1970s	19.0%	11.1%
Average of all equity funds	10.4%	11.7%

Source: *A Random Walk Down Wall Street*[39]

TABLE 5.2. How the top twenty equity funds of the 1980s performed during the 1990s

	Average annual returns	
	1980s	1990s
Top 20 funds of the 1980s	18.0%	13.7%
S&P 500 Index	14.1%	14.9%

Source: *A Random Walk Down Wall Street*[40]

TABLE 5.3. How the top twenty equity funds of the 1990s performed during the 2000s

	Average annual returns	
	1990–99	2000–09
Top 20 funds of the 1990s	18.0%	-2.2%
S&P 500 Index	14.9%	-0.9%

Source: *A Random Walk Down Wall Street*[41]

So if past results aren't indicative of future results, what else is there to rely on? You may want to invest only with an Ivy League-educated, energetic, polished, and intelligent-speaking investment professional, but this would defy logic because many portfolio managers and top advisors have many of the same traits. Usually from an upper-middle or high-class demographic, many advisors have completed university degrees and obtained the industry-gold-standard CFA designation. Except for slight nuances, talking to an investment professional from New York would be similar to talking to one from London, Mumbai, or Toronto. Let's face it—portfolio managers are such primarily because they've met the licensing requirements, come from good socioeconomic backgrounds, present well, and look the part. Although anomalies persist, investors would be hard-pressed to find a plethora of portfolio managers who came from lower-class demographics. One is pretty much the same as the rest, from a bird's-eye view.

Information, Fundamental Analysis, and Technical Analysis

Weather forecasters have a lot in common with portfolio managers. Weather forecasters have access to a great deal of information through real-time data, graphs, satellites, technical instruments, and more. Yet despite this, I can't tell you how many times actual weather conditions differed from their forecasts. Some days called for rain, but instead there was sunshine. Similarly, portfolio managers have access to a great deal of information and techniques, including historical and real-time data, graphs, valuation models, and fundamental and technical analysis. However, like weather forecasters, portfolio managers are subject to various outcomes that may or may not reflect their original projections.

The information advantage that investment professionals once enjoyed over unprofessional investors has declined dramatically over the past several decades. All investors are generally more informed, with greater access to information. As this information gap continues to close, professionals will find it more challenging to take advantage of information that was once shrouded in mystery. For example, through many discount brokerages, investors can access insider buy/sell reports. Legal *insider trading* stipulates that key company personnel must report their activities within a given time frame. Who better an indicator of company prospects than company executives, who have a vested interest in the results? This report, along with other insightful information, was harder to obtain decades ago, but now it is commonplace and highly accessible to interested parties. The Internet has also democratized investment information, and in many ways it's become a great equalizer. Countless websites offer real-time prices, up-to-date information, news alerts, opinions, reports, and more for free or for a fee. Investment professionals such as portfolio managers still enjoy having access to company management and sophisticated software, but outside of that, their information superiority simply isn't what is used to be. All investors can create and enjoy solid information ecosystems to yield sound decision making.

Fundamental and technical analyses are useful but incomplete. Naturally, these methods lead to greater insights about where and how a company is positioned. However, these methods can never be a source of complete reliability for two major reasons: They are exposed to subjectivity, and the future is unknown. If there were an objective truth or "true value" of a security, then in theory, all market participants would align to the same truth, but in reality we know that's not the case. Portfolio managers, like many market participants, make judgment calls and speculate while forecasting a security's future price. For example, while one manager believes Company XYZ's earnings will increase by 10 percent during the next twelve months, a different manager believes earnings will increase by 8.5 percent. Estimates always conclude with a portion of participants beating, meeting, or missing the numbers.

Technical analysis faces the same subjective issues as fundamental analysis. Because technical analysis is focused primarily on the interpretation of charts, technicians' opinions will vary. It's unrealistic to think that many technicians would be aligned to seeing the same patterns while they're emerging at exactly the same times. Even if there were a strong consensus, it would be difficult for everyone to capitalize on the same opportunities at once because the market would change rapidly to reflect feverish activity.

An additional limitation of security valuation techniques is that they cannot incorporate unknown or future information. This may sound obvious, but how many investors stop to think about it? I'm sure many of us, including myself, have been surprised by a company news update that was contrary to our prior assumptions. For example, sometimes a company will surprisingly announce a lowered sales forecast, product recall, accounting irregularities, or management reorganization. Our most thorough research can't include possible future events, and therefore, the true value of a security remains forever elusive, even to the best of us.

Scorecard

Many Americans and especially the media are obsessed with results, performance indicators, and statistics. For example, sports coverage and political races are infused with real-time information highlighting stat leaders, scores, poll numbers, and probabilities. The endless barrage of numbers can actually get quite nauseating for viewers. Portfolio performance is something always on the mind of investors because their future depends on it. Investors pay fees for resources such as advisory and portfolio management services, newsletters, and analyst reports in the hopes of producing positive outcomes. Results should be linked to three professional categories: the investment analysts who cover corporate activities, mutual fund "experts" who provide investors with advice, and portfolio and hedge-fund managers who manage assets. These professionals have ample access to information and resources to make excellent decisions, so let's explore their track records.

Investment Analysts

Investment analysts collect and analyze financial statements, economic forecasts, trading volumes, history, and other sources of information. Their analysis is made available to other market participants to aid financial and investment decision making. Based on projections, models, opinions, and research, analysts strive to produce summaries and estimates regarding companies' future prospects. Each earnings season, publicly traded companies report their earnings results. Companies in the S&P 500 receive the lion's share of focus due to their impact on financial markets and the economy. Actual earnings and other key performance indicators are compared against consensus estimates, which are figures based on the combined estimates of analysts covering those respective companies. Often you'll hear in the daily business roundup that a company met, missed, or beat estimates relative to their consensus. Approximately thirty analysts cover some stocks, while other stocks have fewer analysts, but either way, it's interesting to see how analysts perform given their placement in the investment community.

A Bloomberg article titled "Analysts' Accuracy on US Profits Worst in 16 Years"[42] describes the results of investment analysts. When the article was written in 2008, analysts' accuracy in predicting US profits had dropped to its lowest level in sixteen years, since Bloomberg began compiling the data in 1992. According to the Q2 results that year, 6.7 percent (67 per 1,000) of analysts' estimations matched reported results. Accuracy peaked in the fourth quarter of 2000, which at best meant analysts got it right 30 percent of the time. Interestingly enough, that same year, the Regulation Fair Disclosure stipulation, known as Reg FD, was adopted. Introduced by the SEC, the Reg FD rule mandated all publicly traded companies to disclose material information to all investors at the same time. Believe it or not, some investors (often large institutional investors) received pertinent market information before others (often smaller retail investors). It appears that the few analysts who got it right may have benefited from selective disclosure (or rubbing shoulders) to assist with their forecasts.

Mutual-Fund Experts

Although primarily focused on accumulating client assets, selling, and relationship building, investment representatives also focus on investment strategy to maximize client wealth. Unlike analysts and investment managers, investment advisors sift through information that tends to be more low-level and less analytical, especially if they sell only mutual funds. There is no official record on how investment advisors perform against benchmarks, but a contest conducted by *The New York Times* featuring the performance of prominent mutual-fund experts was quite revealing. In 1993, *The New York Times* enlisted five mutual-fund experts to create hypothetical portfolios, starting with $50,000 for someone who planned to retire in twenty years.[43] The benchmark for their portfolios would be the S&P 500 index, alluding to a passive investment strategy. The result was that none of these five high-profile financial experts and their portfolios outperformed the market over the initial seven-year period, as evidenced in Figure 5.4. In fact, according to Morningstar Inc., only 21.4 percent of the 990 actively managed domestic diversified equity funds in its database outperformed the S&P 500 index over the same period.[44] With so few funds outperforming the index, it's a wonder why so many financial advisors promote actively managed funds.

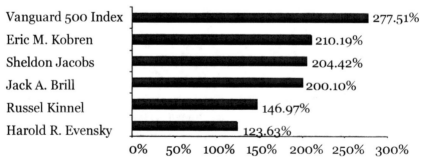

FIGURE 5.4. How the west was won—results of mutual-fund experts' hypothetical portfolio management

Portfolio Managers

One of the best and most comprehensive reports measuring *portfolio management* performance is called the Standard & Poor's Index versus Active (SPIVA) Scorecard. Produced by Standard & Poor's, the report is designed to provide an accurate and objective comparison of how active portfolio managers perform versus their appropriate style benchmarks, correcting for factors that have skewed results in previous index-versus-active-analyses in the industry. The report has gained momentum since its inception in 2001 and has spread to other countries such as Canada, Australia, and India. The SPIVA report makes great efforts to ensure that the comparison metrics are level, adjusting for what's known as *survivorship bias*. Survivorship bias is the tendency for mutual funds with poor performance to be dropped by mutual fund companies, generally because of poor results or low asset accumulation. Many poor-performing funds are closed and/or merged into other funds to shove poor results under the rug. Naturally this is an important issue when analyzing past performance because some mutual-fund companies seek only to promote those funds that are doing well. Unlike other commonly available comparison reports, SPIVA Scorecards account for the entire opportunity set, not just the survivors, thereby eliminating survivorship bias.

While the Dow Jones is the most cited index in the media, the S&P 500 index is the most cited for performance comparisons. Other countries may refer to the S&P 500, but they may also defer to their local indexes for comparisons. The annual percents indicated in Table 5.4 show the number of active managers who *underperformed* the S&P 500 index. For example, in 2010, 61.8 percent of active managers who competed against the S&P 500 index failed to beat it; conversely, only 38.2 percent outperformed it.

TABLE 5.4. Active management versus the S&P 500

Fund category	Benchmark	2009	2010	2011	2002–2011 average
All large-cap funds	S&P 500	50.8%	61.8%	81.3%	59.4%

Source: S&P SPIVA Scorecard Year-End 2011[45]

Although bonds receive less coverage regarding the index-versus-active debate, results have been much worse than those for equities. In fairness, however, there is less performance equality because some bond benchmarks aren't fully replicable. Table 5.5 shows results from December 2001 to December 2011, with percentages indicating how many portfolio managers underperformed.

The SPIVA report also highlights other reasons why investors may choose active management—for example, for small-cap and bear-market management. The compelling argument is that less information and coverage engulfs small-cap companies and, as a result, portfolio managers should have the ability to exploit opportunities not available in the efficient and information-saturated large-cap environment. According to S&P, "Indexing continues to be much more deeply entrenched in the US large-cap market than the US small-cap market. However, over the last decade, SPIVA Scorecards have consistently shown that indexing works as well for US small caps as it does for US large caps."[46] Table 5.6 confirms as much, indicating the number of active managers who underperformed the S&P SmallCap 600 index. For example, in 2011, 85.8 percent of active managers underperformed the index; conversely, only 14.2 percent outperformed it.

TABLE 5.5. Active management versus bond benchmarks

Fund category	Benchmark	2001–2011 average
Government intermediate funds	Barclay's Int Gov't Bond	91.71%
Government long funds	Barclay's Long Gov't Bond	68.43%
Government short funds	Barclay's 1- to 3-Year Gov't Bond	71.09%

Source: S&P SPIVA Scorecard, Year-End 2011[47]

TABLE 5.6. Active management versus the S&P 600

Fund category	Benchmark	2009	2010	2011	2002–2011 average
All small-cap funds	S&P 600	32.2%	63%	85.8%	63.1%

Source: S&P SPIVA Scorecard, Year-End 2011[48]

Finally, just like believing in Santa Claus or the tooth fairy, it's nice to think that under bear-market conditions and market panic, active managers will be around to deliver the goods. After all, they can "move money to cash" or seek "defensive positions" to lessen exposure to market risks. It makes perfect sense to perform these activities, but to have that much foresight, accuracy, and market-timing fortitude requires a crystal ball that is hard to come by. According to S&P, "In the two true bear markets the SPIVA Scorecard has tracked over the last decade, most active equity managers failed to beat their benchmarks."[49] Table 5.7 shows that 83.8 percent of active managers underperformed in the small-cap category in 2008.

TABLE 5.7. Active management in bear markets

Fund category	2000–2002	2008
All large-cap funds	53.5%	54.3%
All mid-cap funds	77.3%	74.7%
All small-cap funds	71.6%	83.8%

Source: S&P SPIVA Scorecard, Year-End 2011[50]

Hedge-Fund Managers

Investors surfing the financial web are bound to come across pictures and profiles of hedge-fund managers. Usually their profiles consist of how much they're supposedly worth and/or how much money they manage, which is often in the billions. Hedge-fund managing is marketed as being an exclusive product for the uber-rich. To join this investment club, investors are asked to ante up a million dollars minimum, usually for a lock-in period of one year or longer. These managers use various nonconventional investment strategies like long/short, market neutral, global macro, and arbitrage. These strategies give them the potential to generate returns in both bull and bear markets, while traditional portfolio management doesn't have the same flexibility.

According to a *Businessweek* article titled "Hedge Funds Lag behind a Generic Stock/Bond Mix"[51], hedge funds weren't doing better than their counterparts. The main Bloomberg hedge-fund index, which tracks 2,697 funds, fell -2.2 percent a year in the five years ending June 30, 2012. The Vanguard Balanced Index Fund, which has a 40/60 split, gained 3.5 percent annually, while the S&P 500 gained 0.2 percent over the same period. The same Vanguard fund also has beaten the HFRX Global Hedge Fund Index, a measure of hedge-fund performance, every year since 2003.

Similar to other active-management endeavors, excellent hedge-fund managers do exist, but a higher investment minimum isn't a guarantor of success. In fact Simon Lack, who spent many years studying hedge funds at JPMorgan, calculates that hedge-fund managers have kept around 84 percent of profits generated, with investors getting only 16 percent since 1998.[52] With a multitude of strategies to implement, it seems the best strategy is to charge clients a 20 percent performance fee on top of a 2 percent management fee.

Eight-Hour Summary

One of the most successful stock pickers in history, Warren Buffet, has frequently stated that investors should seek passive investment strategies. According to Buffet, "A very low-cost index is going to beat a majority of the amateur-managed money or professionally managed money. The gross performance may be reasonably decent, but the fees will eat up a significant percentage of the returns. You'll pay lots of fees to people who do well and lots of fees to people who do not do so well."[53]

This chapter is about which investment strategy makes more sense. A timely Tweet by SmartMoney reads as follows: "Over past decade, 57% of fund managers failed to beat benchmark indexes after fees. Last year, 84% underperformed."[54] The breadth of information available along with SEC mandates has closed the gap between small and large investors, which is why, in part, portfolio managers are losing their edge. Other valuation tools such as fundamental and technical analyses are useful, but their projections are nonetheless in the eye of the beholder. Today, passive management is the out right winner, but if logical active-manager selection methods surface and performance odds later point to them, then let's reconsider. Unsavvy investors are what Dr. Phil would refer to as "enablers" of active management. Active management shouldn't be eradicated, but it also shouldn't be attracting more assets than passively managed solutions. Despite the results of investment analysts, experts, and investment managers, we should still thank them for their efforts in keeping valuations realistic. Without them, the markets would truly be random and would become a gambler's haven.

In the book *The Magic of Thinking Big*, David J. Schwartz says, "The successful are active" and "The just average, the mediocre, the unsuccessful are passive."[55] Maybe it's this line of reasoning that propels the notion of employing financial advisors and portfolio managers to add value. The notion that someone is "looking out for you" and actively making decisions sounds more promising and damn right sexy compared to accepting market returns. Perhaps owning stocks that brokers have hand-picked is better for water-cooler talk than owning five index funds.

However, the primary goal of investing is to gain returns that allow investors to fulfill their current and future lifestyle. The goal is not necessarily to "beat the market." The securities that make up index funds are determined indirectly by millions of investors, whereas securities of actively managed funds are selected directly by a few decision makers. The chances of a few decision makers outsmarting the masses is often small, and although some active managers have reason to celebrate, it's likely that their luck or skill will eventually run out. Passive management leverages the countless minds of those buying and selling the securities that make up those indexes. In essence, by index investing, investors are putting many people to work in the pursuit of finding "true values."

VI
Everyone is Kung Fee Fighting

Unnecessarily transferring wealth to advisors in fees and expenses does not favor those who desire riches.

I hate going to the dentist. I've been visiting dental offices ever since I was a little boy for annual checkups. Despite having healthy gums and teeth, seeing the arsenal of dental tools always makes me feel very uncomfortable. When I was young, my parents asked (forced) me to go. Although I'm no longer forced to go, I set up regular appointments voluntarily. My teeth have never given me any problems, which could be attributed to luck and the care of dental professionals. Dentists must complete a lot coursework and examinations to become licensed, not to mention the thousands required in tuition fees. However, like any profession, there are good and bad dentists. Good dentists have similar traits that apply to successful professionals in other industries, whereas bad dentists share traits with those who are not successful in other industries. Either way, I've decided that attempting to become a DIY dentist isn't in my best interest, and given the high enough dental-industry standards, I'm delighted to receive their expertise in exchange for a fee. The fees I pay them lead to results. Fees, compensation, and taxes are married to investing, and they're unavoidable wealth-erosion factors. Fees and compensation facilitate a financial industry composed of products and services so that investors have wealth-building solutions to choose from.

Fees, compensation, and tax details, unlike the future performance of an investment strategy, are available up front. Investors shouldn't focus on paying fees per se, but rather how much they pay in fees for the value they receive. Following is a list of fees that may or may not apply, depending on the guidelines provided by a financial institution.

Applicable Fees

Account & Administration

This fee is basically to keep an investment account open, and it's usually an annual fee—for example, forty dollars. Many financial institutions waive this fee once an account rises above a minimum amount of assets. Some financial institutions also may waive the fee if the investor accepts account statements online rather than by hard copy. In any case, this relatively small fixed charge becomes less meaningful as assets increase over time.

Trading

Buying or selling securities attracts a fee, which ranges from one brokerage firm to the next. Trades can be executed online, by phone, and with a broker's assistance, with the related charges increasing in the same direction. Promotional teaser rates are often available for a limited time. Some firms waive trading charges for certain types of securities such as ETFs, or they may offer preferred rates for making a certain number of trades per time frame—for example, three months.

Margin

Some investors invest using borrowed money, which is referred to as "buying on margin" or *margin investing*. Margin investing provides many loan ratio options, such as 1:1, 2:1, or 3:1. For example, a 1:1 ratio enables investors with $50,000 to borrow up to $50,000 for investment purposes. A margin loan is subject to interest charges, an expense that should be deducted from gross portfolio performance. Those same interest charges, however, may be tax-deductible. Margin investing carries additional risks because gains and losses are amplified compared to cash-only investing. Do your homework and evaluate several margin-investing scenarios before attempting this type of investing.

Managed-Fund Fees

Managed-fund fees are stated by a *total expense ratio* (TER) or "expense ratio." An expense ratio represents ongoing expenses that cover portfolio management, distribution, and other operating costs. It's stated as a percentage—for example, 1.75 percent—and the TER is paid directly from the fund's assets, thus indirectly from fund investors. Figure 6.1 lists typical managed fund expenses, along with a percentage example. Moving clockwise, investment management fees are .55 percent and so forth. The total expense ratio for this hypothetical fund is 1.75%.

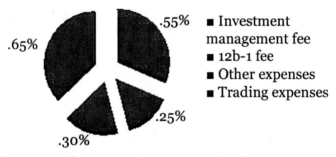

FIGURE 6.1. Sample expense ratio breakdown

Investment/Portfolio Management Fee (.01 – 1.00 percent)

An investment management team that actively manages a fund is compensated for ongoing analysis, selection, and allocation of securities. Passively managed funds also have portfolio managers, but these funds track traditional indexes, so fewer investment activities take place, resulting in lower management compensation. An investment management team can consist of as few as one or two portfolio managers, but it can expand to include traders, analysts, and sales personnel.

12b-1 (.25 – 1.00 percent)

12b-1 is a distribution charge that provides a way for investors to pay indirectly for some or all of the services they receive from investment representatives. 12b-1 fees also can be used to pay for a fund's advertising and marketing expenses, but they are primarily used to compensate advisors and other financial intermediaries for assisting investors before and after they purchase funds.

Other Expenses (.01 – .50 percent)

Other expenses cover administration, operational, custodial, shareholder, legal, accounting and transfer agent expenses. This fee acts as a catchall category for items that are not related to investment management or 12b-1.

Trading Expenses (.10 – 3.00 percent)[56]

Portfolio managers incur trading costs any time they buy or sell securities, and fund investors pay for these costs. These expenses are difficult to find and less transparent from one fund to the next because they are not included in a fund's expense ratio. The best place to find these expenses is to look in a fund's prospectus or to inquire with the firm directly.

Third-Party Licensing Fee (.01 – .15 percent)

Mutual and exchange-traded funds bearing the names of popular index creators such as S&P, Dow Jones, MSCI, NASDAQ, or Russell pay for the use through licensing fees, which are embedded in an expense ratio.

Performance Fee (10 – 20 percent)

Hedge-fund managers are well known for taking large cuts from profits in addition to charging investment management fees. Hedge-fund managers usually set a performance benchmark or *hurdle rate* to exceed — for example, 5 percent — with any returns above the hurdle rate being subject to a performance fee. This differs from traditional portfolio-management compensation, whereby portfolio managers do not operate on a performance-fee basis.

Opportunity Cost

Opportunity cost isn't a fee, per se, but it's the opportunity you forgo by selecting one alternative over the other. For example, an investor chooses to invest in an actively managed fund over an index fund. The returns are 5 percent and 7 percent, respectively. The investor lost out on the opportunity to make 2 percent by choosing the actively managed fund.

Impact of Fees

Many investors are unaware of the impact fees have on returns. Fee information tends to be buried in prospectuses and ill prioritized on investment company websites. Due to the lack of fee transparency, it makes it difficult for investors to consider the component parts of expense ratios. Industry and market participants have a habit of blurring the terms *performance* and *returns*. These terms should not be used interchangeably because each describes a different part of the gain/loss equation. *Performance* is what the market or fund achieves before expenses, inflation, and taxes. The *return* is what the investor has gained or lost after expenses and furthermore when inflation and taxes have been accounted. Let's say that, in a given year, the market is up 7 percent, which indicates performance. If active management underperforms the market by 1 percent, the fund delivers a 6 percent performance, not the higher market performance. By deducting erosion factors, we can calculate the fund's return. The fund's expense ratio is 2 percent. Inflation erodes the value of money, so it, too, is a critical factor that we'll estimate at 2 percent. Tax calculations aside, many investors focus on pre-tax returns versus the more important after-tax results. The final result is a net return of 2 percent before taxes, as detailed in Table 6.1. All else equal, the more investors pay out in fees, the less they keep in returns.

TABLE 6.1. Performance and return

Market performance	7%
Fund performance	6%
Expense ratio (−)	2%
Inflation (−)	2%
Net return (pre-tax)	2%

The above scenario illustrates the impact of fees and other factors over the course of one year. However, many investors invest for longer terms, so by comparing the impact of fees over a period of time, we can better evaluate various outcomes. We also can factor in passive and active investment strategies. According to the Investment Company Institute (ICI), actively managed equity funds averaged a .93 percent expense ratio in 2011 (which doesn't include potentially hefty portfolio-management trading expenses). Index equity funds averaged a .14 percent expense ratio.[57] Both averages could be adjusted by considering the fees paid to advisors, but for simplicity's sake, we'll start with comparing the average expense ratios without them. Tables 6.2 through 6.5 each feature an initial investment value, twenty-year time horizon, rates of performance, expense ratios, and net rates of return. The "Difference" column represents the dollar difference between the total returns.

TABLE 6.2. Impact of average expense ratios

	Passive	Active	Difference
Initial value	$250,000	$250,000	
Years of growth	20	20	
Performance	7.00%	7.00%	
Expense ratio	0.14%	0.93%	
Net rate of return	6.86%	6.07%	
Total	$942,417.64	$812,440.17	$129,977.47

TABLE 6.3. Expense ratio increased by 1 percent for management trading expenses

	Passive	Active	Difference
Initial value	$250,000	$250,000	
Years of growth	20	20	
Performance	7.00%	7.00%	
Expense ratio	0.14%	1.93%	
Net rate of return	6.86%	5.07%	
Total	$942,417.64	$672,224.99	$270,192.65

TABLE 6.4. Active management outperforms market by 1 percent

	Passive	Active	Difference
Initial value	$250,000	$250,000	
Years of growth	20	20	
Rate of return	7.00%	8.00%	
Expense ratio	0.14%	1.93%	
Net rate of return	6.86%	6.07%	
Total	$942,417.64	$812,440.17	$129,977.47

TABLE 6.5. Active management underperforms market by 1 percent

	Passive	Active	Difference
Initial value	$250,000	$250,000	
Years of growth	20	20	
Rate of return	7.00%	6.00%	
Expense ratio	0.14%	1.93%	
Net rate of return	6.86%	4.07%	
Total	$942,417.64	$555,202.10	$387,215.54

Each of these scenarios demonstrates the significant impact of fees can have on long-term gains. Table 6.4 gave a 1 percent performance advantage to active management, but you would need to outperform the market consistently by at least your fees to keep pace with passive investing results. Although passive investors aren't immune to inflation and taxes, reduced expense ratios are beneficial cost-control measures.

Advisor Compensation

Investment representatives can be beneficial to investors under the appropriate compensation agreements. It's a matter of understanding the value an advisor adds versus the cost of performing activities personally.

In most cases, it's in your best interest to learn how to manage your own investments. The more you dole out in compensation, the fewer returns you have to hold onto. Similar to active managers, advisors don't have crystal balls that can lead to consistently outperforming the market, as we've seen with the best of them. Rather, advisors act as a middle man between investment solutions and investor needs. They rely mainly on their salesmanship and ability to develop trust among clients. Keep in mind that advisors, as pleasant as they are, have primary goals to generate new business and increase their income.

Advisors may use one or multiple compensation models such as commission, fee-based, fee-only, and salary. Compensation type, for the most part, is dictated by the two main advisor platforms: broker–dealer and investment advisor. On the broker platform, registered representatives generally engage in transaction-based, commission-based, and sales-load compensation. On the investment advisory platform, fee-based and fee only are more commonplace.

Commission-Based Advisors

The commission model dominates the broker landscape. The client doesn't receive a bill or invoice, but rather compensation is deducted upon purchase or by using a deferred payout structure. Representatives who use the commission approach charge what's called a *load*, which is separate from the 12b-1 fee. Load-share classes include front-end, back-end, level, and none, and, like expense ratios, loads are represented by a percentage — for example, 5.75 percent.

- *Front-end loads* (Class A) generally charge a sales commission at the time of purchase. Investment fund companies usually set a maximum front-end load that can be charged.
- *Back-end loads* (Class B) compensate advisors through a combination of one-time, contingent deferred sales loads (CDSL) and annual 12b-1 fees. The CDSL compensation is contingent on investors remaining in a fund for a specified period of time. This is a method of compensating advisors indirectly, but if investors exit a fund before the specified period ends, they will be charged a CDSL percentage. The CDSL percentage decreases throughout the investment holding period and typically reaches zero after the shares have been held for approximately seven years. After seven years, back-end load shares usually convert to a share class with

lower 12b-1 fees. For example, Class B shares will typically convert to Class A shares after a specified number of years.
- *Level-load shares* (Class C) compensate financial advisors with a combination of lower CDSLs (often 1 percent) and annual 12b-1 fees. Similar to the back-end-load model, investors do not pay commissions up front, but shareholders will pay should they sell their shares within a specified time period.
- *No-load share classes* do not charge sales commissions but may have 12b-1 fees of 0.25 percent or less. Investors can purchase no-load funds through employer-sponsored retirement plans, mutual-fund supermarkets, discount brokerage firms, and bank trust departments, as well as directly from investment fund companies. Some investment companies may offer a fund class that omits fees paid to advisors using fee-based models.
- Investment advisors may use a *commission* model whereby they charge a fixed percent or amount per trade such as 2 percent or fifty dollars, respectively. This commission structure is usually found at full-service brokerages, with investment advisors licensed to sell mutual funds, stocks, bonds, derivatives, and ETFs.

Fee-Based Advisors

Fee-based advisors charge a fixed percentage for *assets under management* (AUM). The percentage they charge may decrease as assets increase, either by performance and/or deposits. For example, an advisor charges her client 1 percent on $100,000 of assets for compensation of $1,000 during one year. When the client reaches $500,000, the advisor will decrease the fee to .85 percent. An interesting caveat to fee-based compensation is the amount paid by clients. If Client A pays $1,000 in compensation for $100,000 of assets under management and Client B pays $2,000 for $200,000, is Client B getting more in services and execution for her additional $1,000? The answer is likely no, which leads to why the next compensation model may be more suitable.

Fee-Only Advisors

Fee-only advisors charge a fixed hourly rate or annual flat fee that varies depending on the services rendered. Fees are not dependent on transaction or assets held. Hourly rates range from $100 to $300, while annual fees vary.

Salaried Advisors

In this model, an employer determines advisor compensation in the form of annual or hourly dollar amount.

Conflicted Advice

For a movie marathon night featuring Wall Street shenanigans, I recommend *Wall Street, Inside Job* (documentary), *Margin Call*, and *Boiler Room*. These four films showcase an industry driven by profits and carelessness and occasionally resemble reality. It's a reality that many investors are unaware of. It consists of conflicts of interest that exist—between salesmanship and stewardship, for example. Some advisors, regardless of their ethical mandates, will place client welfare above compensation, no matter what. Other advisors will focus primarily on compensation while barely meeting the needs of their clients. It's amazing that Warren Buffet and other prominent investment experts recommend passive investing, yet there is an army of advisors who aggressively sell compensation-centric, actively managed solutions to investors. To highlight the uncertainty regarding advisor conduct, a study by the Staff of the US Securities and Exchange Commission found the following: "Many find the standards of care confusing, and are uncertain about the meaning of the various titles and designations used by investment advisers and broker–dealers. Many expect that both investment advisers and broker–dealers are obligated to act in the investors' best interests."[58]

This confusion is part of a growing concern regarding advisor conflicts of interest. Investment advisors have a fiduciary duty to serve the best interests of their clients, including an obligation to relegate their interest behind their clients' interest. Investment advisors who have a material conflict of interest must either eliminate that conflict or fully disclose the conflict to their clients. On the other hand, brokers generally are not subject to the same standard of care and fiduciary duty under federal securities laws. Their focus isn't the client's best interest, but to a lesser degree carrying out fair dealings concerning client suitability and recommended solutions. Broker-registered representatives outnumber investment advisors by two to one. That means that two out of every three advisors are potentially seeking commission-based compensation, which could lead to compromised advice. According to wealth management consultant and lecturer Steven Blum, "Unfortunately, the typical 'financial advisor' does not come close to meeting the standards of practice that most clients really need. There is a natural conflict of interest between a financial advisor and client. The financial services industry was built on a system of paying commissions, which is still the primary way most advisors make their money. The result is a terrible conflict between the financial advisor and the client: The former wants to make as much money as possible while the latter desires the wisest solution."[59]

Steven Blum's statement isn't without merit and can be supported by a study regarding financial advice given to retail investors. The study sought to answer the question "Do financial advisors undo or reinforce the behavioral biases and misconceptions of their clients? The study found that advisors encourage what the study calls "returns-chasing behavior" and that advisors push for actively managed funds that have higher fees, even if clients start with low-fee, well-diversified portfolios. According to the study[60], "We find that advisers have a dramatic bias towards active management. In nearly 50% of the visits the adviser suggests an actively managed fund, whereas in only 7.5% of the advice sessions advisers encourage an investment in an index fund. Moreover, though advisers mention fees, they do so in order to downplay it. For example, they often say 'this fund has a 2% fee but that is not very much above the industry average.' Their responses to the different portfolios reinforce these facts. They are broadly supportive of the trend-chasing portfolio but unsupportive of the index fund portfolio."

You should verify which type of investment representative you have so that you can ensure alignment with your investment needs. FINRA is the largest independent regulator for all securities firms doing business in the United States. Its website contains a lot of useful information. Of particular interest is the ability to get background information on advisors. BrokerCheck is a free search tool to help investors research the professional background of current and former FINRA-registered brokerage firms and brokers, as well as investment advisor firms and representatives. Advisor profiles highlight current and past registration, employment details, and qualifications.

Financial advisors are no different than salespeople who sell real estate, fridges, or cars. All non-salaried sales professionals whose compensation is tied to productivity seek to generate the highest amount of income while best satisfying a client's need. If a customer needs a fridge with certain specifications, an appliance salesperson will try to match those needs, preferably selling the fridge with the highest price tag to maximize his commission. Commissions are also just the tip of the iceberg. Additional incentives may include sales bonuses, company awards, and vacations that can lead to further conflicts. Similarly, if a client requires exposure to US equities through a mutual fund, a commission-based advisor will seek to fulfill that request while potentially seeking the highest associated payout. In this scenario, both advisor and client goals are met, but the client may not have received an unbiased recommendation. The SEC has done very little to change compensation practices, but the Financial Services Authority (FSA) of the United Kingdom and the Australian Securities and Investments Commissions (ASIC) both imposed bans on commission-based compensation.[61,62] The reasons for doing so focus on placing clients' interests first, improving transparency, and reducing inappropriate advice. The bans are meant to promote better-quality advice, market competitiveness, expense ratio reductions, and fewer rogue advisors.

Fifty Shades of Conflict

More than anything else, conflict goes deeper than the investment advisor and broker platform. It boils down to an advisor's character and ethics. You'll have commission-based advisors who may be limited to offering only mutual funds yet rigorously consider fund profiles so that they can recommend the best product. Investors may work with fee-based investment advisors who have fiduciary duties to clients but who recommend products based on investment-firm relationships. Finally, fee-only or salaried advisors may be conflicted between keeping client assets versus instructing them to use the money for alternative purposes such as paying down a mortgage. Conflict may never be completely absent, but your goal is to work with advisors who present the least conflicted advisory model. Here are a few signs that an advisor may have a conflict of interest:

The advisor recommends managed funds from only one investment company. Considering how many investment companies there are and the number of managed funds that exist, why would an advisor recommend products from only one investment company? Compensation aside, it could also be a matter of business or personal relationships, complacency, convenience, or lack of due diligence. It's rare that one investment firm is highly successful in every investment category, so client portfolios should reflect multiple firms unless FoFs or TDFs are used.

The advisor has you in too many funds. An allocation of five to seven funds provides ample diversification. Fewer funds are legit when using broad-based indexes, FoF, or TDF, but more than seven funds should raise a red flag. Advisors could be rotating funds into back-end loads to generate new commissions off old money. In addition, these advisors may not understand allocation principles and diversification.

The advisor does not discuss or offer index-based investments. Most advisors are unaware of how poorly active management performs against indexes for starters, but those who are aware may still focus on selling actively managed funds because of the convenience the commission model provides. Every advisor should be reviewing with his or her clients the advantages and disadvantages of both investment strategies.

The advisor limits compensation to a commission-based model. Advisors who provide investment services through commissions only are inherently conflicted due to the limitations of their compensation philosophy.

The advisor does not discuss or recommend fixed-income investments. Fixed-income securities should be in every portfolio, even for the most aggressive investors. However, some advisors purposely keep fixed-income exposure to a minimum to attract higher compensation from equity fund sales.

The advisor promotes excessive buying and selling. Known as *churning*, advisors sometimes engage in excessive trading on behalf of clients as a means to increase commissions. Advisors may be instructing trades frequently or through discretionary authority, conducting a high degree of portfolio turnover. A warning sign of churning is an unusual increase in transactions without portfolio gains, especially during times of low market volatility.

Taxes

It pays to understand tax law or to hire someone who does. Taxes play an integral role in investment strategy and bottom-line results. It applies to all facets of investing. Pay particular attention to after-tax returns, portfolio turnover, and non-taxable vs. taxable accounts. Investors who aren't well versed in tax planning should seek the services of tax specialists or financial planners who have tax expertise.

After-Tax Returns

After-tax returns seem to get overlooked in an industry that focuses on everything but. The best and fairest assessment of returns is to use after-tax results as a common denominator. Consider for a moment the tax rules applied to capital gains, dividends, or interest. The tax rate on short-term capital gains, assets held for one year or less, could range from 10 to 35 percent. For example, an investor realizes a gain of $5,000 on $50,000 invested within one year. The $5,000 represents a pre-tax return of 10 percent, but if subjected to a 20 percent capital gains tax, the resulting pre-tax gain is reduced to $4,000 for an after-tax return of 8 percent.

Portfolio Turnover

Active management is in the business of buying and selling securities. *Portfolio turnover* is an indicator of how often securities within a fund are bought and sold by the managers. A high portfolio turnover rate will lead to high transaction costs and may result in higher taxes when investments are held in taxable accounts.[63] On the other hand, index investing, due to being passively managed, experiences very little portfolio turnover, if any, within a given year. Therefore, index investors are less likely to experience capital gains compared to actively managed products. For example, a fund reports a 20 percent turnover rate, which means that one-fifth of the securities (20 of 100) in the portfolio were bought and/or sold. A portfolio with a turnover rate of 20 percent indicates that the fund manager holds a stock an average of five years. In general, passive strategies have lower turnover rates, and fund managers who trade frequently have a higher turnover rates.

Non-Taxable Accounts

Non-taxable accounts such as an IRA or 401(k) allow investors to defer paying taxes on capital gains, dividends, and interest. This is a great benefit because investments can grow and compound without being diminished by annual taxes. An equal comparison could be made between trees that continually grow due to warm temperatures versus trees that die due to cold temperatures, only to start growing again the following year. There are slight nuances, advantages, and disadvantages regarding the various retirement account options, but when possible, you should use at least a portion of these accounts for investing. Figure 6.2 compares taxable and tax-deferred growth. Starting with $100,000 invested over twenty-five years at an annualized return of 7 percent, the impact of a 25 percent federal income tax rate separates the two amounts by approximately $183,000.[64]

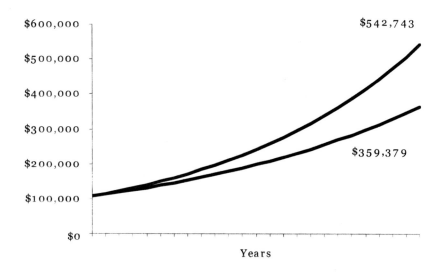

FIGURE 6.2. Taxable and tax-deferred growth

Eight-Hour Summary

Investing isn't free, and associated expenses are meaningful to the overall investing process. The industry and many advisors have ample room to improve fee transparency, disclosure, and investor education, but waiting for them won't help investors optimize their portfolios. Asset allocation is dependent and future performance is unknown, but fee information allows investors to make wise decisions. Various investing scenarios provide insight into how impactful fees can be over the long term. All else equal, common sense should direct actions to securing the lowest cost portfolios while fulfilling investor needs. An important cost consideration is active management and advisor services. Active management is relatively expensive compared to passive management, while passive-performance results seem to be the better bargain. Paying advisors for a random bag of investment choices doesn't make much sense when the alternatives are carefully analyzed. You need to consider seriously the costs, benefits, and value proposition associated with active management and investment representatives. Investment representatives are compensated through various models such as commissions, fee-based, fee only, or salary, which typically relates to their operating platform.

A timely Tweet by The Motley Fool reads as follows: "59% of investors mistakenly believe that "financial advisors" are required to act in their best interest."[65] Brokers are salespeople who provide investment services based on client suitability. Investment advisors provide many of the same services but are legislated to a higher standard of care. Regardless of the platform, you need to ask your advisor one very important question: How do you avoid conflicts of interest? If you suspect that you aren't receiving unbiased recommendations, then you should consider alternatives such as using a different advisor or becoming a DIY investor.

After-tax returns are often ignored but are essential to analyzing investment performance. You should take advantage of non-taxable accounts when possible to allow money to compound by deferring taxes.

VII
DIY Rises

Our potential to learn new things far exceeds our desire to be continually sold.

Becoming a DIY investor is what this book is all about. I cannot emphasize enough that making the transformation will be extremely beneficial to your future lifestyle. Investing can be practical, fair, and simple, or it can be impractical, conflicted, and complex. My goal is to help you create a plan whereby you experience the former. A reasonable time frame for making the transition from advised client to DIY investor is six months to a year. This doesn't mean portfolios will be exactly where they should be, but the time frame will allow you to learn, research, and consider alternatives.

The term "DIY investor" acts as a catchall for all market participants who don't use investment representation. Some so-called DIY investors day-trade stocks, while others focus on derivatives. DIY investors differ from DIY traders (or day traders) in that they focus on holding securities long term and passively, while traders focus on profiting from short-term price discrepancies. The investment approach I hope DIY investors adopt focuses on product choice and index investment strategies. However, the first and most important decision investors need to make is how involved they want to get in their investment activities. I have categorized investors into four types to provide a sense of what will be demanded of each. The basis of involvement relates to six factors: time, knowledge, desire, confidence, activities, and rebalancing. The investor types are often blended, and there is something for everyone as outlined in Table 7.1.

Investor Types

Eight-Hour Investor

The eight-hour investor spends the least amount of time on investment activities by using FoFs and TDFs. These investors spend a couple of hours each quarter reviewing their accounts and fund compositions, which is perfect for those with restricted schedules. A basic familiarity of investment and financial concepts, similar to many brokers, is all that is required because investment managers manage the FoF and TDF selections. The desire to stay updated with all things investing isn't really necessary, and confidence in decision making can be average because individual securities are not being selected. Rebalancing and transactions are kept to a minimum because the investments pretty much take care of themselves.

Fund Investor

The fund investor sticks with managed funds but delves deeper to build a portfolio consisting of five to seven funds focused on specific categories. Many of the same characteristics resemble those of an eight-hour investor except that fund investors may have to do research on certain fund choices. For example, selecting a large-cap US fund isn't that much different than selecting a broad-based US fund except for the percentage exposure to all US equities. However, investors who select a health care fund will want to do research on the industry to align with their investment decision. These investors are seeking positive indicators that suggest particular investment categories are likely to beat the general market. Conversely, randomly selecting investment categories isn't a prudent investment strategy. These investors have a desire to get more involved and don't mind the additional rebalancing activities.

Stock Picker

The stock picker desires to build a portfolio of individual bonds and stocks. The demands here are similar to portfolio managers, with the goal of "beating the market." A minimum of forty securities will suffice as long as they represent a cross-section of industries for diversification. In an effort to select forty securities, the stock picker analyzes a minimum of two hundred securities (likely a lot more), spending four hours on each. Knowledge of financial statements and fundamental analysis is required, along with a strong desire and confidence to navigate through the markets. Rebalancing and transactions will be much more frequent, causing the expense ratio and fees to increase.

Trader

Finally, the trader isn't really an investor per se and is focused on short- to mid-term price movements. Much is borrowed from the stock picker profile except that successful traders tend to focus narrowly on a handful of securities. Each security traded requires at least one hour of follow-up per week. The intricacies of trading require greater knowledge than the other investor types to increase the probability of success. The trader is very similar to a portfolio or hedge-fund manager who uses various analysis methods to identify buying and selling opportunities. The trader requires a strong desire and confidence to deal with investment minutiae.

TABLE 7.1. DIY investor types

	Eight-hour investor	Fund investor	Stock picker	Trader
Investment selection	FoFs and TDFs	Investment category funds	Individual securities	Various securities
Annual time requirement	8 hours or less	8–30 hours	800 hours minimum	52 hours minimum
Knowledge	Average	Average	Above average	Above average
Desire	Low – mid	Mid	High	High
Confidence	Average	Average	Above average	Above average
Activities	Analyze fund holdings	Analyze fund holdings and industry reports	Analyze various statements	Analyze various statements
Rebalancing	Low	Low – mid	High	High

DIY Investor Benefits

DIY investors enjoy many benefits that advised clients do not. For starters, most advisors don't seek to help their clients become financially literate. Rather, advisors focus on salesmanship and ongoing relationship development to keep clients around. These activities have devastating financial implications because financial literacy is what promotes a person's wealth. The client–advisor model also interrupts the wealth-creation process due to unnecessary fees that erode returns and transfer wealth to various stakeholders involved in the investing process. Here is a summary of a few key DIY investor benefits.

Empowerment

There is nothing like being highly engaged and in control of making intelligent investment decisions. While many investors will continue to outsource their investment literacy and decision making to "trusted" advisors, DIY investors are confident and come full circle to appreciate the investment process. They lead a purposeful investment agenda and seek to make the most out of their money.

Knowledge

There is a lot of information out there, but most of it's trivial. Investors already know that markets will move up and down on any given day, week, month, or year. They know that some days will seem better or worse than others. They know that a chorus of media professionals is employed to report daily minutiae. However, none of this impacts DIY investors because they understand investment mechanics.

Independence

Why squander money on services you can perform yourself? Most advisors spend six to ten hours annually managing investor accounts while getting paid handsomely to do so. Self-sufficient, disciplined, and interested investors can find the time to manage their own affairs. DIY investing actually frees up more time because back-and-forth communication, travel, and meetings are eliminated.

Reduced Fees

One of the reasons Amazon.com is able to offer products at lower prices than other retailers is because it bypasses the traditional distribution channel, which consists of various intermediaries who *margin-pinch*, increasing the price until it finally reaches the consumer.

The traditional distribution channel looks like this:

Manufacturer > agent/broker > wholesaler > retailer > consumer

Amazon's distribution channel looks like this:

Manufacturer > Amazon (retailer) > consumer

The same logic applies to investors who pay more by using the traditional client–advisor model. For example, consider investors who use the services of mutual-fund representatives. On average, investors pay between 1 and 2 percent, or $1,000 to $2,000, per $100,000 invested. By bypassing the advisor and active portfolio manager(s), a DIY investor focused on indexing can limit fees to a fraction of a percent. Expense ratios for index funds can be as low as .05 percent, or $50 per $100,000.

The typical client–advisor model looks like this:

You > advisor > dealer/brokerage > portfolio manager(s) > investments

The DIY investor model looks like this:

You > discount brokerage > investments

Increased Returns

When your portfolio dipped during the tech bubble, housing crisis, or other event, what did your advisor do for you? Did she pick the exact moment to enter and exit the market? Of course not because investment professionals don't have crystal balls, and studies show that few consistently beat the market over the long term. As an investor, you should worry less about performance and focus more on returns. Low expense ratios and portfolio turnover associated with index funds increase the chance of receiving higher returns.

Four Reasons to Bid Your Advisor Adieu

Right before you make the decision to become a DIY investor, you're going to hit a stumbling block. You are going to hear about returns some advisors got for their clients or come across articles that read "DIY Investors: Don't Go It Alone." Let's take a second to be truthful. Part of being an adult means being accountable and responsible. From getting married to having children, a career, and a home, life is about making and owning up to those decisions. There are services that laypeople need, but investing isn't one of them. It's unfathomable that so many adult investors bow to the bullhorns of Wall Street without giving pause to the extremely important topic of money. The value proposition of investment representatives is to help fulfill financial and lifestyle goals. They are to provide sound investment advice, keep investors informed, and educate them on financial matters. In an ideal world, this would be the case, but due to conflicts of interest and sales targets, the application of sound investment strategies gets lost in the mix. Investors in advised-client models are really paying for a false sense of security and shunning personal accountability. The time is now to become a DIY investor. Say this statement with me: "I've evolved, I'm accountable, and my hard-earned dollars won't be squandered any longer. Much potential wealth has been shed, but I'm ready to take control."

There are several reasons why you don't need investment representatives, as follows:

1. Low Barrier to Entrance

Compared to the daunting demands and countless hours of study required by dentists, lawyers, doctors, or actuaries, becoming an investment representative is extremely easy. The Series 6 exam qualifies individuals to sell mutual funds and costs $95 to write.[66] The Series 7 exam qualifies individuals to trade various securities and costs $290.[67] Combined with another inexpensive series exam (63 or 65); pass a multiple-choice exam, complete some registration paperwork, and presto—a person is qualified to tell people how to invest their money. With such low standards, just about anyone can become an investment representative.

2. Goal Misalignment

Remember, the goal of advising is to make money (and plenty of it) while satisfying client needs. However, satisfying client needs isn't the same as optimizing their needs. This brings rise to conflicts of interest that favor the advisor, depending on how savvy or unsavvy the client is. It's amazing that approximately 90 percent[68] of investors are invested in actively managed funds, yet index funds have proven to be the smarter investment strategy. Perhaps advisors are to blame for their recommendations, or maybe investors who lack knowledge and accountability are at fault.

3. One of Many

I know that when advisors send holiday cards, birthday e-mails, or must-read articles to clients, it makes the investors feel all warm and fuzzy inside. Those are nice gestures that convey care and interest to make the client feel well taken care of. However, for seasoned veterans, a client is one of many clients being taken care of. With only so much time available, advisors designate a status or letter grade of A, B, C, or D to indicate the client's importance and future revenue-generating potential. There is nothing wrong with great service and salesmanship, but I wouldn't be satisfied being one of many. On the flip side, there are thousands of advisors. Investors use advisors out of convenience or by way of referral. Most investors fail to see the industry as a whole, with many salespeople doing business all over, gunning to manage money.

4. Market Direction Unknown

My crystal ball tells me the markets will continue to move up and down no matter who I pay to manage my money. Therefore, it makes sense to take on the responsibility myself so that I pay fewer fees and increase the probability of higher returns. This is far better than hearing the usual spiel: "The markets have gone through a rough patch, but things are starting to look up." It's foolish to employ others who have no say or control over an entity such as the financial markets. We've also seen the "best" experts underperform the markets, similar to their portfolio-managing peers.

When it's time for you to notify an advisor that his services are no longer required, he may or may not try to keep you from leaving. Sometimes this is when advisors start to show they care, but their reaction often depends on how much income they make from you. Nonetheless, if the advisor unleashes an arsenal of tactics to keep you from becoming a DIY investor, that is when you should explain that you would like to attempt investing on your own and that you'll stay in touch. If you have had a very positive client–advisor experience, you also may want to add that you'll still refer business to him.

Six Steps to DIY Status

One of the biggest challenges for budding DIY investors is where to start. DIY freedom isn't an overnight process because it entails a few definitive steps taken over a period of months. Some market participants think it's easy to turn a quick buck, but the markets don't benefit those who continually use shortcuts over the long term. Like any process, an understanding should lay the groundwork to accomplish activities effectively. The first five steps are covered in this chapter, and the sixth step is covered in the next chapter. Figure 7.1 illustrates the six steps.

FIGURE 7.1. Steps taken to DIY status

Step 1 — Improve Investment Literacy

Countless books, magazines, blogs, infomercials, and other media create a confusing environment. The confusion often leads to investors quitting before they start. Let's face it, the reason advisors are hired is due to the perception that they have knowledge and skills superior to everyday people. Because they can't predict market movements, the only knowledge they have is based on understanding market activity and investment terminology. In addition, advisor licensing exams tend to be institutionalized and generic. They're less likely to include objectivity and thorough analysis on topics such as active versus passive management or the impact of fees.

The goal of investor education is to keep things simple and practical. By reading books, investors learn about investment concepts, terminology and strategies. Blogs, magazines and social media are learning extensions that are used to create an investment literature ecosystem, as illustrated by Figure 7.2. As extensions, these resources should be sought after only when a sound knowledge base has been solidified through old-fashioned book reading. Many books are available on a range of investment topics such as day trading, options trading, hedge-fund management, and the list goes on. However, our goal is to gain a solid understanding about investing and managing investments with as much ease as possible and having the type of portfolio that requires only a few hours a year to manage.

Books

To get the most out of reading, it helps to employ active reading strategies, which can increase your level of engagement and your absorption of new concepts. Naturally, there will be some overlap and repetitiveness of concepts, but it's a good thing when respected investment authorities are singing the same chorus. To make the most of your reading efforts, here are a few strategies to try:

- Make notes or comments in the margin instead of using a highlighter.
- Identify and look up the definition of any unfamiliar terms.
- E-mail yourself a few new and interesting chapter concepts.
- Read each paragraph carefully and then determine what it says and what it "does."

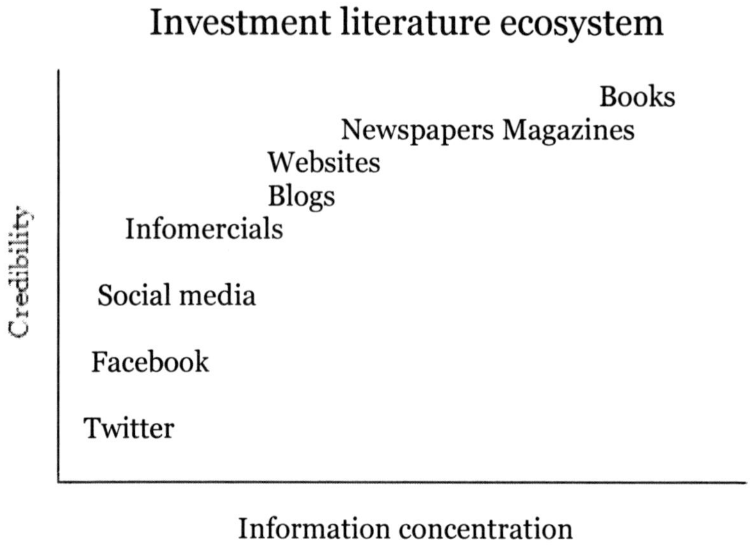

Investment literature ecosystem

```
         |                                    Books
         |                      Newspapers Magazines
         |                  Websites
         |                    Blogs
Credibility |      Infomercials
         |
         |     Social media
         |
         |    Facebook
         |
         |    Twitter
         |_____
                    Information concentration
```

FIGURE 7.2. Investment literature ecosystem

- Write a chapter summary in your own words.
- Teach what you have learned to someone else.
- Reread paragraphs and concepts you don't understand the first time.

Books by or on John Bogle, Burton Malkiel, Warren Buffet, Peter Lynch, and Benjamin Graham all have merit. Books range in content from beginning to advanced, so reading can be a trial-and-error activity. If a book is too simple or too complicated, try another. As I mentioned, my favorite book is *A Random Walk Down Wall Street* written by Burton Malkiel. It's one of the most influential books on the subject of stock markets and all things investments. It provides a well-rounded understanding of various matters, including bubbles, portfolio construction, analysis methods, and more. For individual stock selection, *One Up on Wall Street* by Peter Lynch is a great choice. In this easy-to-read book, Lynch outlines a practical approach for choosing stocks based on his successes and failures.

Newspapers and Magazines

Daily newspapers and magazines are wonderful resources for staying updated. Some add legitimate value, while others don't, but neither will have as much impact on forming a knowledge foundation as books. Newspapers will provide the occasional educational series, but for the most part, their focus is on reporting daily financial news bites. Personal finance magazines can be of great value because they can help reinforce principles and provide insightful perspectives. Note that offline resources may provide an online equivalent for free.

Online Resources

The online environment, consisting of websites, blogs, and social media, can be a healthy and beneficial part of the learning process. There are a lot of financial minutiae that are irrelevant to investing, so you must extract the worthwhile elements. Exposure to online resources isn't for the purpose of acting on every whim, but rather to stay aware of market activity and the investment landscape. For example, when you see an article that reads "Top Ten Stocks to Own Right Now," the goal isn't to buy those ten stocks but to read the article for interest's sake. You also will come across various advertisements and subscription offers, many of which won't add value, so buyer beware. Naturally, my online recommendations suit my personality and interests, but other investors may desire something different. Whether you are considering websites, blogs, or social media, as you stumble upon options, consider the following attributes:

- Objective—Are differing opinions as well as pros and cons being presented?
- Fact-based—Do the author's opinions derive from due diligence, research, and thorough analysis?
- Insightful—Is the information current and forward-thinking?
- Qualified—What qualifies the individual(s) or company to speak about investment matters?
- Realistic—Is the author stating unrealistic investment goals, promising results, or making impractical statements?
- Free of conflict—Is there any reason to believe that the author's opinions and recommendations have a hidden agenda?

Recommendations

Investopedia is one of the best, if not the best and most comprehensive, investment website dedicated to investor education. Investopedia is a resource for financial terms, personal finance, articles, tutorials, and more.

www.investopedia.com @Investopedia

The Motley Fool champions shareholder values and advocates tirelessly for the individual investor. Their products and services are designed to help people take control of their financial lives.

www.fool.com @themotleyfool

MarketWatch covers several topics such as investing, spending, borrowing, and planning. It's part of *The Wall Street Journal* digital network, which is under its parent company, Dow Jones & Company. Of particular value are their how-to guides regarding stocks, ETFs, and other securities.

www.marketwatch.com @MarketWatchPF

Morningstar is a leading provider of independent investment research. Its website provides insightful articles and excellent tools for analyzing securities. Although this site isn't directly focused on investor education, it is very investor-friendly and helpful.

www.morningstar.com @MorningstarInc

Bloomberg is a leading provider of financial and business news. Its website offers frequent market updates and insightful perspectives on many investment facets and sectors. Similar to Morningstar, the site isn't focused purely on investor education, but for those looking for a constant stream of reliable information, there is no equal.

www.bloomberg.com @BloombergNews

Step 2—Set Goals

Financial and lifestyle goals work hand and hand. Naturally, people use money for all sorts of things that result in their current and desired experiences. Their experiences define their standard of living and include the car they drive, the food they eat, the places they visit, and the activities they engage in. Many of us desire more money so that we can expand and improve our lifestyle options. Consider a person seeking a higher salary (financial) so that she can upgrade her car (lifestyle). Few people have a crystalline vision of what they'll be spending their money on a month from now, never mind in retirement. While individuals in their twenties may not be prepared to define their financial and lifestyle goals, people should definitely get a sense of their goals before it's too late. Their expectations don't have to be 100 percent accurate, but general ideas about lifestyle needs and wants should be considered.

Although needs and wants are synonymous, separating the essentials from the nonessentials will help you further define goals. By tracking and budgeting, you can get a good idea of your annual income requirements. For example, Bob and May are in their fifties and live a very frugal yet enjoyable lifestyle. They've downsized to a modest home, travel once a year, and play a few rounds of golf together. Their month-to-month expenses roll up to annual income needs of $70,000 before taxes. Knowing their annual expenses and making a few adjustments, Bob and May have planned their future around their annual income needs.

Pre-retirement or retirement lifestyles may attract less, more, or equal expenditures than perceived. Financial targets tend to be less of concern while you're employed because employment income is used for current needs. But in retirement, employment income will be replaced by other sources such as the government, a company pension, savings, and investments. Either way, tying dollar amounts to current and future lifestyle expectations is how financial goals are shaped. Lifestyle considerations pretty much remain constant throughout life, starting with a place of residence. Where and how people live will likely have the most impact on their finances. Other considerations such as standard of living, basic needs, transportation, travel, memberships, entertainment, and activities will be influenced by an accumulated nest egg. Children returning home can be a factor when considering pre-retirement or retirement years.

Financial goals have the ability to influence asset-allocation decisions. As you figure out your retirement budget and compare it with your current financial resources, you will have more than, less than, or just enough to fulfill your lifestyle expectations. For example, a conservative investor who's facing a projected shortage of income has ten years until retirement. He may have to consider a slightly more aggressive portfolio in the hopes of gaining more returns to close the gap. Alternatively, he could consider reducing his projected retirement needs while maintaining his investor profile by planning to live in a less costly residence, for instance.

Step 3—Create an Investor Profile

As you make decisions about your investor profile, those decisions will influence your asset mix. We know from previous chapters that an investor profile is based on various factors such as age, investment objectives, time horizon, risk tolerance, and knowledge. Additional factors such as net worth, annual income, employment status, investable assets, and future investments also should be considered. Investor profiles lie at the core of investment behavior and decision making. Advisor–client relationships usually go though the process of determining an investor's profile, which can be helpful to reference. You also may want to consider your personality and character in general terms to determine whether you are someone who is conservative or more of a risk taker. There are no hard and fast rules about which investor profile category to choose; it comes down to being comfortable with the risk/reward profile of each category. As your investment knowledge and experience increase, you may keep or change your profile as you see fit.

Profile considerations can be grouped together based on age and/or years to retirement, as we saw with life-cycle investing. Because we know which factors are used to develop a profile, drawing conclusions about such factors will be an effective way to start. Each criterion in Table 7.2 is denoted by a letter as it relates to the investor profile categories: (G) growth, (B) balance, or (C) Conservative. All else equal, these notations signify general guidelines regarding an investor's life cycle. For example, a sixty-one-year-old investor seeking capital preservation is better suited toward a conservative asset mix and not growth. Conversely, consider an investor who falls in the age range of twenty-five to forty-four; she may choose to implement a conservative portfolio, although her years to retirement provide ample time to implement a growth asset mix. She does this because she has a low risk tolerance and does not want to be subject to huge swings in portfolio values.

TABLE 7.2. Investor profile considerations

Factor			
Age	25–44 (G)	44–59 (B)	60+ (C)
Objective	Accumulation (G)	Income (B)	Principal protection (C)
Time horizon	7+ years (G)	3–7 years (B)	1–3 years (C)
Risk tolerance	High (G)	Medium (B)	Low (C)
Knowledge	High: Could speak comfortably with Warren Buffet about investments.	Medium: Knows the differences between stocks and bonds.	Low: Wouldn't be able to find at least ten companies in the Dow 30.

New investors may want to meet with an advisor for the purpose of discussing investor profiles. As a DIY investor, the goal is not to seek advisory services but simply to gain more perspective. Completing an online investor profile questionnaire also can be insightful. Another option is to start investing conservatively until a desire or need stimulates a profile change. There is no universally accepted standard for asset-allocation models, but common sense would dictate that models should differ enough to be easily distinguishable. Given the factors above, there are several models available for each age range, as shown in Table 7.3. Asset model percentage splits describe the amount of fixed income to equity. The equity option includes all other securities that are not fixed income, such as REITs, derivatives, and alternative investments, but these allocations still should be detailed.

TABLE 7.3. Fixed-income to equity allocation models based on age

Age	Very conservative	Conservative	Balanced	Growth	Aggressive growth
25–44	80/20	65/35	40/60	30/70	20/80
44–59	85/15	70/30	50/50	35/65	25/75
60+	90/10	75/25	60/40	40/60	35/65

At the account level, investors often have different profiles to suit their account objectives—for example, growth for a 401(k) but very conservative for an emergency savings account. To prevent profile misalignment, the sum of the account profiles should reflect your overall profile. Let's say an investor is comfortable with a balanced profile equating to a 50/50 split. If he has several investment accounts such as a 401(k), retirement, and a taxable account, the sum of those accounts should be in close alignment with the 50/50 weighting, as depicted in Table 7.4.

TABLE 7.4. A balanced profile reflecting multiple accounts

Account	Value	Fixed income	Equity	Split
401(k)	$50,000	$25,000	$25,000	50/50
Retirement	$25,000	$15,000	$10,000	60/40
Taxable	$10,000	$ 2,500	$ 7,500	25/75
Total	$85,000	$42,500	$42,500	50/50

Step 4—Establish Guiding Principles

DIY investors are on their own, which doesn't have to be a scary endeavor as long as you follow a few principles. Whether you realize it or not, you already have guiding principles relating to work, relationships, and life in general. Perhaps your work principles include refraining from gossip or attending meetings on time. Your relationship principles may include returning e-mails within 24 hours and contacting friends at least once a month. When using advisors, investment principles are less of a priority because advisors dictate principles on behalf of clients. But DIY investors will want to create a few guidelines to reference for future decisions and behavior. An investment principle could be something like ensuring that a portfolio's expense ratio is less than half a percent. Another principle could be refraining from acting on hot investment tips. The idea is to list several rules that will guide you on your way to investment discipline and success. If you are entirely new to investing, you might want to make a list that contains a couple of principles to get started. The principles are in your hands and will change as you gain more knowledge, experience, and comfort.

Here are a few worthy principles with additional considerations to follow:

- Select index funds that provide ample diversification—e.g., a minimum of 30 securities.
- Manage a portfolio consisting of a FoF, TDF, or three to seven low-fee index funds.
- Keep my portfolio's expense ratio at less than half a percent.
- Keep active management and individual security selection to a minimum—e.g., less than 10 percent.
- Do not invest in securities that I don't understand or couldn't explain to someone else.
- Keep exposure to financial news and daily activity to a minimum to reduce unnecessary noise and trivial information.
- Subscribe to one magazine and follow one blog.
- Read one investment book annually.
- Don't participate in IPOs or act on unqualified recommendations.
- When adverse swings in the market take place, review my portfolio and make the necessary changes to bring asset class weightings back into alignment.

Other Guiding Principles

Ego

Avoid trying to time the market, which has been a futile activity for the majority of investors. Who is anyone, including you, to pick the exact moment to buy and sell? Consider the investment climate, fundamentals, and how possible decisions will affect your goals, investor profile, and guiding principles.

Execution

Always consider the bigger picture and think through investment decisions before executing. Carefully analyze securities to validate buying or selling opportunities.

Emotions

Don't let your emotions get the better of your investment activities. Avoid reacting to market volatility, economic downturns, and negative sentiment. Follow a rebalancing plan.

Resources

Act as a steward of resources and seek to plant seeds that will grow into healthy money trees. Invest what's available, and don't invest what you can't afford to lose.

Engagement

Stay on top of things and follow through with investment duties. This doesn't mean paying attention to the news 24/7, but rather periodically reviewing your portfolio.

Guidance

Don't be afraid to ask for help, no matter how big or small the detail. The source of guidance should be unbiased, transparent, trustworthy, and value-added.

Step 5—Develop an Investment Policy Statement

An investment policy statement (IPS) is an account-level document that combines elements of the investor profile and guiding principles. It goes a step further to address account specifics using verbal statements and includes additional considerations such as the account profile, monitoring, and asset allocation. Similar to asset-allocation models, there isn't a universally accepted IPS layout, but basic components are found by comparing one to the next. High fee brokerages will issue fancy IPSs that contain twenty pages or more, but this document need not be longer than two pages. The main IPS sections include account profile, monitoring and review, asset allocation, and an "other" section, which is optional.

Account Profile

Account profile is the first section of an IPS and includes the following items:

- Account (choose one): 401(k), IRA, 403(b), 457, 529, taxable, other

- Objective: Define the purpose of the account—e.g., to preserve capital, income, or growth. Investors also may want to provide a label such as "retirement" or "travel account."

- Risk tolerance: Define risk tolerance for the account, which should closely relate to the allocation defined in the investor profile document. State how often the asset mix will be reevaluated to ensure that it aligns with your comfort level and overall investor profile. If applicable, state why the asset mix has been allowed to deviate from the core allocation—for example, from conservative to growth.

- Time horizon: State a possible retirement date and estimate how much money should be accumulated, annual income needs, withdrawal rate, and other considerations regarding investment requirements.

- Reinvestment policy: Will you reinvest dividends, interest, or capital gains distributions? By which method? Check, electronic transfer, manual withdrawal, or other?

Account types are available for various investment objectives—for example everyday use, retirement, and college savings. The differences regarding accounts center on contribution limits and tax guidelines. Table 7.5 lists some of the most common types of accounts.

Monitoring and Review

Monitoring and review is the next section and includes the following:

- Rebalancing: Define the asset class and investment category deviation minimums that will trigger rebalancing activities. As a general rule using five to ten percent for deviation minimums is fine. For example, when the fixed-income weighting moves by more than 10 percent, it will be time to rebalance. State when rebalancing will take place if necessary—i.e., quarterly, semi-annually, or annually.

- Performance tracking: State how often performance will be reviewed—i.e., monthly or quarterly.

TABLE 7.5. US account descriptions

Account	Description
Taxable account	A taxable account that permits individuals to set aside money each year for various objectives
IRA (individual retirement account)	A tax-deferred retirement account that permits individuals to set aside money each year, with earnings tax-deferred until withdrawals commence
Roth IRA	An individual retirement plan that bears many similarities to the traditional IRA, but contributions are not tax-deductible, and qualified distributions are tax-free
401(k)	A qualified plan established by employers to which eligible employees make salary deferral (salary reduction) contributions on a post-tax and/or pre-tax basis
Roth 401(k)	An employer-sponsored investment savings account that is funded with after-tax money
403(b)	A qualified plan similar to a 401(k) but is offered by nonprofit organizations such as universities and some charitable organizations rather than corporations
457	A non-qualified, deferred compensation plan established by state and local governments, tax-exempt governments, and tax-exempt employers
529	A tax-deferred savings plan designed to encourage saving for future college costs, including tuition, room and board, and other expenses

Asset Allocation

Asset allocation is the third section and includes the following:

- Investment strategy: Passive (P) ____ percent, active (A) ____ percent

- Asset allocation: Cash ____ percent, bonds ____ percent, equities ____ percent, alternatives ____ percent

- Investment vehicle: Select which security or combination of securities you will use to manage your portfolio.

Security	%
Mutual funds	
ETFs	
Individual stocks	
Individual bonds	
Alternatives	

In the client–advisor world, asset-allocation investment details are usually found on an IPS along with a nice-looking pie chart. However, the DIY investor will find it much easier to manage allocation details using spreadsheet software such as MS Excel.

Other

You may want to add an "other" section to your IPS to address issues like how often you'll search for new products, account conversion or critical dates, contribution amounts, or notes for future actions.

DIY Investor: Jennifer Stevens

Jennifer Stevens, 44, has used the services of an advisor for more than ten years. The advisor approached her by way of referral from one of Jennifer's close friends. Service has been good, with emphasis on two-way communication and excellent follow-up. However, recently Jennifer came across an article highlighting the differences between passive and active management, the associated fees, and performance results. This motivated her to learn more about her investments rather than continuing to take a sleepy-eyed approach to outsourcing her financial responsibilities.

Jennifer didn't want to make any rash decisions, so she decided to maintain her current advisor while she learned more about investing. As she developed her investment savvy, she came to appreciate many facts about the investment world. For starters, she realized that her good client–advisor relationship involved more salesmanship than stewardship because her advisor had recommended only actively managed investments without discussing alternatives. Jennifer also did some basic calculations and realized that a small spread in expense ratios leads to dramatically different outcomes. In addition, she realized that asset allocation doesn't have to be that complicated; after all, decisions are based on three main categories: cash, bonds, and stocks.

Step 1—Improve Investment Literacy

Jennifer's investment research thus far has included a few articles and newspaper clippings. Jennifer committed to reading three investment books and visited Amazon.com for her potential reading list. She drilled down to Books > Business & Investing > Investing > Introduction and sorted by relevance. Basing her book choices on the number and quality of reviews, she selected *Eight-Hour Investor, A Random Walk Down Wall Street,* and one other book. Jennifer designed a reading plan to ensure that she reads her books in a timely fashion.

Step 2—Set Goals

Jennifer considered her long-term goals and the lifestyle she wants in retirement. She articulated these goals on paper and attached dollar values to them to get a rough idea of how much she'll need annually in retirement. Jennifer is confident about her financial and lifestyle assessment, but she decided to meet with a fee-only financial planner to get some more ideas and information regarding the bigger picture.

Step 3—Create an Investor Profile

Jennifer considered her general life tendencies and state of mind during past financial crises. She also considered her client–advisor investor profile and decided that she is a balanced investor. She considered her age, financial targets, objectives, time horizon, and risk tolerance.

Step 4—Establish Guiding Principles

Jennifer adopted several guiding principles that derive from the books she's read and her life experiences.

Step 5—Develop an Investment Policy Statement

Jennifer created a one-page IPS for her IRA account that reflects her overall investor profile, guiding principles, and account objectives.

Jennifer's DIY Investor Profile

DIY Investor:	Jennifer Stevens
Age:	44
Objective:	Preserve capital 10 percent, income 40 percent, growth 50 percent
Desired rate of return:	7 percent
Time horizon:	10+ years
Risk tolerance:	Medium
Knowledge:	Medium
Core profile allocation:	50/50
Asset split considerations:	70/30, 65/35, 60/40, 55/45, 50/50, 45/55, 40/60, 35/65

Guiding DIY Principles

- Manage a portfolio consisting of three to seven low-fee index funds.
- The indexes should be broad-based to provide ample diversification.
- The portfolio's total expense ratio should be less than .45 percent.
- Refrain from active management and the selection of individual securities.
- Subscribe to a monthly personal finance magazine.
- Don't participate in IPOs.
- Read two investment books a year.
- Review my guiding principles annually.

Jennifer's Investment Policy Statement

Account Profile
Account: IRA

Objective: To grow assets using equities while lowering portfolio volatility by balancing with cash and bonds. Account is for future retirement income.

Risk tolerance: My risk tolerance is balanced. I will revaluate my asset mix every three years to ensure that it aligns with my comfort level and overall investor profile.

Time horizon: My target retirement date is 2032. I expect to have an estimated net worth of $1,200,000 in today's dollars that will supply an annual pre-tax income of $60,000 until age eighty-four.

Reinvestment policy: I will reinvest distributions in the form of dividends, interests, and capital gains where eligible.

Monitoring and Review
Rebalancing: I will rebalance my portfolio when an asset class exceeds 10 percent and when an investment category exceeds 10 percent. Rebalancing will take place quarterly if necessary.

Performance tracking: I will review and record my portfolio's performance semi-annually.

Asset Allocation
Investment vehicle: 100 percent ETFs

Investment strategy: Passive management 100 percent, active management 0 percent

Asset allocation: Cash 10 percent, bonds 40 percent, equities 50 percent

Other
Security selection: I will review ETF alternatives every two years and consider replacing existing choices.

Eight-Hour Summary

DIY investors want to optimize and insulate their wealth prospects. DIY investors can reduce fees and increase returns as well as become empowered, knowledgeable, and independent, putting themselves in the driver's seat. The traditional client–advisor relationship has, for the most part, become obsolete as it relates to portfolio management. The old model was once applicable when portfolio management was shrouded in mystery and access to information was limited to the rich and powerful. However, all that has changed with easy-to-understand investment literature, blogs and websites, newspaper articles, and other information generally being highly accessible, unlike in decades gone by. Comprehensive financial advice still has some application and benefit. However, the DIY investor understands that most investment-only representatives are unlikely to beat the indexes consistently while absorbing relatively high fees. Therefore, with a disciplined passive management and product-centric approach, DIY investors will be better positioned to fulfill their long-term financial goals.

There are different profiles that allow investors to determine their level of ongoing engagement. You can find success by selecting a FoF, TDF, or a few funds, or you may pick individual securities. The critical factors to consider are time, knowledge, desire, and confidence. There isn't a right or wrong investor type, nor does one guarantee better results than the other; it's a matter of how much energy you want to expend on investment activities.

The recipe for becoming a DIY investor is actually very simple. Start with financial literacy to create a lifestyle vision, then move on to an investor profile, guiding principles, and policies to follow. The process can be quite liberating. Each step should also act as part of a feedback loop so that investment activities can be refined to yield better results. Investing doesn't have to be a complicated activity anymore than shopping, getting gas, or cleaning out the garage. It's a matter of commitment, improving financial literacy, and planning the road ahead with those factors you know are in your control.

VIII
Let's Dance

You and only you should be the steward of your investments.
Your lifestyle and future depend on it.

Exploring literature will improve the odds of successful investing. By tying in lifestyle and financial goals, you gain greater perspective concerning the activities you must accomplish. The investor's profile and guiding principles initiate a framework in which to carry out those activities. The investment policy statement lends itself to rounding out the six-step process by making decisions about investment strategy and allocation. Whereas the previous steps involved mostly documented decision making, step six, developing an action plan, implements IPS decisions that complete the DIY investor transformation. Developing an action plan focuses on the timing of events, as well as detailed portfolio construction, selecting investing intermediaries, and portfolio monitoring. In short, this is where the fun starts.

Making the Transition and Fees

Timing and fees are two important factors budding DIY investors should consider. Investors may be faced with the task of altering their portfolios. The timing of buying and selling securities may have tax consequences and should be discussed with a tax professional. Investors should be prepared to review their current portfolios and intentions. It's also beneficial to ask the tax professional what documentation will be useful in preparation for a meeting. Another aspect of timing relates to an investor's current priorities. Perhaps the investor is in the midst of a career change or planning to change residences. Take stock of what's going on and decide if the timing is right to make a transition. Investors with lump sums to invest should consider the market environment and their investment allotment plan. Even though investors may have a long-term horizon, spreading out purchases may be more beneficial for *dollar cost averaging* (DCA) purposes. DCA is a purchasing technique that applies a fixed dollar amount at regular intervals to a particular investment, regardless of the share price. For example, an investor has $40,000 to invest but decides to invest $10,000 in a TDF quarterly. More shares are purchased when prices are low, and fewer shares are bought when prices are high. Without DCA, investors are subject to an ill-timed lump-sum purchase at prevailing market highs.

If you have invested in mutual funds through an advisor, by selling those funds you may be subject to redemption and/or load penalties. It's extremely important to understand the current status of mutual-fund investments. **I repeat: It's extremely important to understand the current status of mutual-fund investments.** The investments may or may not have come off the back-end or level load schedule. You can find out this information by calling the fund company or speaking to your advisor. Investors who don't inquire may be subject to financial penalties that would automatically reduce the value of their investments. Transferring "in-kind" or "in cash" are two options typically given to investors when moving accounts from one brokerage to another. *In-kind transfers* move account holdings as they are, whereas *in-cash transfers* automatically redeem account holdings into cash before the account is transferred (sales charges may apply). This little tidbit is often the angst of many transfers, but if done correctly can save a lot of grief. Transferring accounts internally or externally from one firm to another can take up to several weeks, depending on the firm's operational efficiencies.

Portfolio Construction

Constructing a portfolio is no different than building a house, making a pizza, or putting a puzzle together. Each of those activities requires different components and processes, but all follow a logical sequence of events to get completed successfully. In building a house, usually the foundation is created first, as with a pizza. Portfolio construction considers the investment vehicle that will act as the mode of allocation transportation. For eight-hour investors, it's a matter of selecting mutual or exchange-traded funds, followed by FoFs and/or TDFs. Fund investors will go a bit further to consider the various investment categories that are found in the various asset classes. Weights are then applied to these categories to reflect the investor's profile.

Investment Vehicle

An investment vehicle acts as the investor's mode of transportation through the investment world. There is no right or wrong choice; rather, the security or securities selected depend on the investor type. Managed funds such as index mutual and exchange-traded funds are all most investors need, but investors may opt for individual securities as well. Individual securities and derivatives selection go beyond the scope of this book; thus, I would highly recommend reading material that pertains to that subject. I don't want to discourage anyone from adding individual stocks or bonds to their portfolios, but may I remind you that very few professionals (full-timers) beat the markets consistently, as we've seen. Investors tend to want to buy individual securities for the wrong reasons, like excitement or to feel productive. The primary reason for buying individual securities is to exceed market returns. Therefore, stock pickers must be diligent about their research and processes as predetermined in their guiding principles and IPS. Refrain from buying on gut feeling and hype and start with money that can be lost in case bad decisions are made. My hope is that you adopt passive and index-based funds to make up the core of your portfolio—or your entire portfolio. Whether the funds are index or active, large or small cap, or a combination, funds are an easy way to get instant diversification, are simple to manage, and require less analysis compared to individual securities.

Mutual and exchange-traded funds have different profiles because they are created differently, and they operate and trade differently. FoFs and TDFs mimic their underlying investment vehicle such as a mutual fund of funds mimicking the security profile of a mutual fund. For passive long-term investors, the differences between mutual funds and ETFs doesn't really matter except for the expense ratio because exchange-traded funds, mutual funds, and fund of funds will generally attract more fees, in that order. Another factor to consider is suitability as it relates to investable assets. As a general rule, investors with less than $100,000 should lean toward mutual funds, and those with more than $100,000 should consider ETFs. However, this also depends on how many funds investors plan to use in constructing a portfolio and how often they plan to rebalance. For example, using a fund of funds, two or three funds with very broad diversification will enable you to manage your portfolio efficiently without being affected by investment-vehicle particulars.

The main reasons mutual funds are the preferred investment vehicle for investors with few assets is because they often require low investment minimums, and they can be purchased in fractional units. You can enter the market with a couple hundred dollars because many mutual funds have low initial and ongoing purchase requirements. On the other hand, ETFs trade like stocks, and, as a result, they efficiently trade in *round lots* of one hundred shares. Trading in round lots of one hundred makes the buy/sell order filling process congruent. An *odd lot* is a number of shares less than one hundred (one to ninety-nine). Imagine how inefficient the market would be if it consisted of investors placing buy/sell orders of random odd lots such as 4, 57, 73 and 207. When an odd-lot order is placed, it may attract a higher commission, be filled late, or be rejected by the exchange. So, while mutual funds require a minimum dollar amount, ETFs attract a minimum trading size. For example, an ETF trading at $50 multiplied by 100 equals $5,000 versus a purchase requirement of $500 for an equivalent mutual fund.

Mutual funds can be purchased in fractional units. This is a benefit to investors who wish to put their entire investment allocation to use. As noted, this differs from ETFs because they typically trade in round lots of one hundred. For example, mutual fund ABC is priced at $11.05, and an investor has $250 to invest. The $250 put to full use will buy 22.624 units ($250/$11.05). Being able to buy and sell in factional units also helps investors rebalance closer to exact weightings, whereas round lots do not. Let's say that an investor is about to rebalance her portfolio, and she'll need to sell 50.345 units to bring the equity weighting back to 10 percent. Mutual funds will facilitate the exact amount, whereas this would be an odd lot for ETFs with the fractional unit unaccounted for. Along with investment minimums and fractional units, Table 8.1 lists some other differences between mutual funds and ETFs.

TABLE 8.1. Mutual fund and ETF differences

Factor	Description	Mutual Fund	ETF
Initial investment	Minimum amount required to purchase securities	Low	Varies
Fractional units	Unit or share transaction flexibility	Yes	No
Real-time price visibility	View to fund's real-time value	No	Yes
Disclosure of holdings	Ability to view current holdings	Quarterly /semi-annually	Daily
Short-term selling penalty/redemption fee	Minimum holding period restrictions	Yes	No
Short-selling	Ability to take a position that profits from the fund's value decreasing	No	Yes
Ability to leverage (margin buying)	Ability to use investments as collateral to purchase additional investments	Varies, but usually no	Yes
Order variety	Ability to place orders other than buy/sell such as market, limited, or stop loss	No	Yes

Investment Categories

If choosing to be a fund investor, the next step is to select investment categories for portfolio inclusion. The eight-hour investor can bypass this step, although it's still worthwhile to learn about investment categories because he or she will find them in the composition of FoFs and TDFs. Investment categories fall within asset classes such as cash, fixed-income, and equity. These categories allow investors to make simple or more involved decisions about where to allocate resources. From broad-market funds to specialty funds, investors have a plethora of options to choose from, as shown in Table 8.2.

TABLE 8.2. Investment categories

Asset class	Investment categories
All	Broad market
	Geographic location
Fixed income	Corporate
	Government
	High yield
	Duration
Equities	Market cap
	Sectors
	Style and focus
	Specialty
Alternatives	Commodities
	Miscellaneous

Broad-Market Funds

Broad-market bond and *equity* funds are highly diversified and include many securities across different categories and industries. These funds seek to represent greater than 85 percent of available securities listed in a particular market. For example, the often-cited S&P 500 contains only large-cap companies, whereas the S&P 1500 contains small-, mid-, and large-cap funds representing 90 percent of the total US equity market. Broad-market global and international funds provide worldwide diversification, but many tend to reflect bond or equity holdings of the largest market-capitalized companies.

Geographic Location

There are many investing opportunities the world over that can be accessed easily by managed funds. You can select regions such as North America; developed markets and emerging markets such as Brazil, Russia, India, and China (BRIC); and single countries such as Canada, Germany, or Chile.

Duration, Government, Corporate, or High-Yield Funds

Bond fund durations are available in short (one to five years), medium (five to ten years), and long term (ten-plus years). Government bond funds hold securities issued by the federal and state governments. Corporate bond funds hold securities issued by corporations of varying creditworthiness. High-yield or junk-bond funds hold fixed-income securities issued by corporations that have fallen below investment-grade status.

Market Cap

Stocks fall into one of three categories: large, mid, or small cap. Large-cap companies tend to be well known and covered by the media like McDonald's, IBM, and Disney. Mid- and small-cap companies tend to be lesser known but remain an essential part of a country's economy and business environment. Market cap funds hold securities that fall within the specified market-cap threshold.

Sector

There are ten distinct sectors in US equity markets, and they may consist of one or more industries. For example, the health care sector comprises of two industries: health care equipment, services, and pharmaceuticals; and biotechnology and life sciences. The ten sectors are health care, consumer discretionary, consumer staples, energy, financials, industrials, information technology, materials, telecommunications, and utilities. Sector funds hold securities of those corresponding companies.

Style and Focus

Value funds hold securities believed to be undervalued in price relative to their fundamentals. Conversely, growth funds hold securities believed to have higher capital appreciation and growth potential. Dividend and income funds hold dividend and interest-paying securities.

Specialty

The *specialty* funds category acts as a catchall for many funds that can't find a home elsewhere. Social and ethical funds invest in securities that follow philosophical and moral guidelines. FoFs and TDFs also may reside in this category. Newer investment strategies such a minimum volatility funds seek to hold securities that have proven to be less volatile than others over a period of time.

Alternatives

Funds found in the *alternative* category may have some overlap with those in the specialty category. Commodity and resource funds may hold physical goods, derivatives, and/or stocks of companies that operate in the industry. Their focus may be broad or narrow, depending on the fund's objective. REIT funds hold securities that generate revenue from operating commercial and/or residential real estate properties.

Miscellaneous

Funds in this category deviate widely from traditional fund types, and they may or may not be suitable for long-term investors. Funds in this category may use strategies categorized as leveraged, inverse, spread, volatility, and event-driven.

Weightings

It would be easier if we could see into the future and allocate accordingly, but because we can't, investors have to embrace their investor profiles and corresponding allocation models. Investment categories are no different because they, too, require allocation weights. With broad-market funds, investors get ample diversification, and therefore a generous weighting of 20 to 50 percent would be OK. After all, balanced investors may decide to select two broad-market funds and allocate 50 percent to each. Sector funds provide focused and limited diversification, so giving them the same generous weighting as broad-market funds would be impractical. While some investors might allocate 100 percent to one sector (by all means), limiting sector funds to a 10 percent weighting or less reduces risk dramatically. Should investors decide to construct portfolios using only individual securities, with a maximum target weighting of 2.5 percent each, this will force diversification of forty securities, which is reasonable. If their maximum weighting was moved up to 25 percent, this could result in a portfolio of just four stocks. That's great if the stocks perform well, but it's not so great if one falls to zero overnight, reducing a portfolio's value by 25 percent.

One easy way to gain more insight into weighting investments is to review several FoFs, TDFs, and other managed funds. Investors will notice that in many equity funds, portfolio managers assign single-digit weightings to individual securities. On the other hand, many FoFs and

TDFs assign weightings similar to those shown in Table 8.3.

TABLE 8.3. Weightings guidelines

Asset class	Investment category	Target weighting
All	FoFs and TDFs	50 – 100%
	Broad market	20 – 50%
	Global, region	20 – 50%
	Location: Country	5 – 20%
Fixed income	Corporate	5 – 20%
	Government	5 – 20%
	High yield	5 – 20%
	Duration	5 – 20%
Equities	Market cap	5 – 20%
	Sectors	5 – 10%
	Style and focus	10 – 25%
	Specialty	5 – 20%
Alternatives	Commodities	2.5 – 10%
	Miscellaneous	2.5 – 10%
Other	Individual securities	0 – 2.5%

Fund Companies and Brokerages

Fund companies and investment management firms are the financial institutions responsible for creating investment vehicles such as mutual and exchange-traded funds. There are hundreds of fund companies and thousands of funds that can make the investment selection process confusing, but DIY investors need to focus on only a few. Starting with a few of the most recognized leaders in the industry, Table 8.4 presents a short list of companies that offer multiple passively managed mutual and exchange-traded fund solutions. Some fund companies such as Vanguard and Fidelity offer brokerage services as well.

Fund-company websites don't differ that much from websites of other industries. They have the usual sections like "About Us," "Contact Details," "Links," and "Disclaimers." Many fund companies have "noisy" web pages featuring values pertaining to stocks, indexes, specials, fees, and random people who look like they're investing or have benefited from investing. DIY investors are after fund information such as the funds that

TABLE 8.4. Fund companies

Fund company	Mutual funds	ETFs
Blackrock (iShares)		√
Fidelity	√	
Schwab	√	√
State Street (Spiders/SPDRS)		√
Vanguard	√	√

are available for personal investing. Funds are usually found under "Accounts and Products," "Investment Products," or simply "Mutual Funds" or "ETFs." Funds are often tied to asset classes and investment categories before the choices become visible. Fund information is usually divided among a few tabs, starting with an overview or summary tab, composition or characteristics, price, performance, and fees. Additional information is usually provided with a link to a fact sheet or prospectus. Table 8.5 breaks down the pertinent items and what they mean.

TABLE 8.5. Deciphering fund profiles

Section	Item	Definition
Overview	Strategy or objective	The investment strategy and focus of a fund
	Ticker symbol	Letters used to identify a publicly traded security
	Inception date	The date a fund commenced trading
	Benchmark or underlying index	The index a fund is tracking or attempting to outperform
Characteristics	Total assets	A fund's assets under management
	Style box or category map	Investment style of a fund, usually referencing market cap size and style of investing (i.e., value or growth)
	# holdings	Number of securities held within a fund
	Top holdings	The top ten securities held in a fund by asset size

Characteristics	Country breakdown	Geographic locations where investments are allocated
	Sector breakdown	Sectors where investments are allocated
Price	Last price	The last price traded of a security
	Net asset value (NAV)	A mutual fund's price per share or ETF's per-share value
	Price highs and lows	The price highs and lows during a specified duration (i.e., day, week, or year)
Performance	YTD, 1 Year, 5 Year, 10 Year…	Performance during a specified duration [i.e., month, year-to-date (YTD) or multiple years]
	Yield	A fund's interest or dividend yield
Fees	Expense ratio or management fee	Costs to operate a fund
Other	Distributions	History of fund distributions
	Distribution frequency	When distributions are paid out (i.e., monthly, quarterly, semi-annually, or annually)

Brokerages

A *brokerage* (or broker) is a middleman who brings buyers and sellers together for the purpose of transacting securities. A *full-service broker* employs investment representatives to provide advice, whereas a *discount brokerage* provides no advice. Because discount brokers do not provide advice, their commission rates are far less than their full-service counterparts. The account opening process is fairly straightforward, with documents and instructions usually available online and with the availability of customer service representatives. Once an account is set up with online access, it gives investors an opportunity to explore a broker's investment platform. Exploring the platform for a week or two is a useful exercise because it allows investors to get familiar and ask questions.

Commissions vary across the board among financial institutions. Commissions are often lowered or waived for using the institution's proprietary products, making a minimum number of trades, or having minimum account balances. Investors with lower amounts to invest naturally feel the impact of fees more as a percentage of their assets compared to investors with more money. For this reason, it's important to review and understand the commissions charged under different scenarios. Commissions and fees are one reason, but not the only reason, to select a broker. In fact, there are several reasons why investors may choose one broker over the other.

Customer Service

Customer service is important in the brokerage business, just like any other business. Some brokers offer online chat features and 24/7 service and support. It's important for brokers to hire knowledgeable and well-trained staff to facilitate the investing experience.

Investment Platform

A broker's investment or trading platform features items such as news, account balances, holdings, order entry, quotes, preferences, and other relevant information. A user-friendly environment that's logical and easy to navigate appeals to investors.

Research

Research tools including reports, commentary, and analysis are vital to investors who are seeking a high level of engagement. Brokers may include a decent set of tools for free and charge a premium for more in-depth analysis.

Product Diversity

Investors may want to limit their investment choices to mutual funds, ETFs, stocks, and bonds. However, others may want to trade futures, options, and foreign-exchange (FOREX) securities. Some brokers have every product under one roof, while others have a standard selection.

Service Diversity

Some brokers have morphed by extending their services to banking, credit cards, and billing. These services are additional conveniences weaved into the traditional broker model.

Technology

The increased use of smartphones and tablets has led some brokers to create applications for investors on the go. For passive investors, apps probably don't add much value, but for semi-active to active investors, apps provide an additional entry point.

While many brokers exist, several can easily accommodate DIY investor activities such as Charles Schwab, E-Trade, Fidelity, Scottrade, TD Ameritrade, and Vanguard.

Monitoring

Discount brokers generally provide basic documents like monthly transaction and tax statements. They may or may not provide pertinent account and performance statements that come with the higher fees associated with full-service brokers. This isn't a problem for most investors who have basic math skills learned in elementary school. As long as you understand mathematical functions such as adding, subtracting, multiplying, and dividing, that's all is takes to keep track of your own investments. If math skills need some work, then you may want to hire a qualified fee-only financial professional to help you get started with documentation.

Before you buy or sell securities, it's highly recommended that you pre-plan your transactions using spreadsheet software. This will give you a chance to apply much of the information outlined in this chapter. There are four areas that you need to focus on: asset allocation, performance, rebalancing, and transactions. The numerical values from these areas generally feed into one another, simplifying the recordkeeping process.

Asset Allocation

The asset-allocation tab can start with asset and investment category weightings, followed by the fund name, ticker, expense ratio, and yield as per table 8.6. You may want to include a column to denote passive or active management and the fund's underlying benchmark for reference. To calculate the initial purchase, multiply the target weighting by the total available amount to invest, then divide it by the security's current trading price. For example, $150,000 to invest multiplied by a 20 percent weighting equals $30,000. A bond fund is trading at $85; therefore, $30,000/$85 = 353 shares. Note: You will often face mixed lots, which are a combination of round and odd lots—e.g., 300 round and 53 odd. Another option besides deciding to use mutual or exchange-traded funds is to call the broker to get advice on the treatment of odd lot orders.

Performance

Keeping track of performance and returns will help ensure that your financial objectives are being met. Returns are the difference between the value of an original investment; its current value plus any dividends, interest, or capital gains minus fees; and other expenses. For example, a $1,000 investment has increased to $1,150 plus a $50 dividend for a total current value of $1,200. The transaction fee of $10 is subtracted, decreasing the return to $1,190. Therefore, the net increase of $190 divided by the original investment of $1,000 equates to a 19 percent net return. The original investment is also known as a *book value*, while the current value is also known as a *market value*.

An easy way to keep track of distributions is to list the funds, months of the year, and total sum, with the total sum feeding into the appropriate cell in your spreadsheet. Table 8.7 and 8.8 highlight performance and distribution tracking.

TABLE 8.6. Portfolio asset allocations

Asset class	Target %	ETFs	Ticker	ER %	Yield %
Fixed	40%	Vanguard Total Bond Market	BND	0.10	1.68
Equity	20%	Schwab U.S. Broad Market	SCHB	0.04	1.91
Equity	20%	Vanguard MSCI Emerging Markets	VWO	0.2	0
Equity	20%	Vanguard Global ex-U.S. Real Estate	VNQI	0.35	0
Total	100%			0.16	1.05

Source: Morningstar[49]

TABLE 8.7. Performance tracker

Fund	Book value	Market value	Distributions	Difference	Return
Vanguard Total Bond	$59,509.95	$65,353.00	$201.54	$6,044.59	10.16%
Schwab US Broad	$30,609.95	$27,400.00	$321.65	$2,888.30	-9.44%
Vanguard MSCI Emerging	$29,409.95	$32,501.00	$0	$3,091.05	10.51%
Vanguard Global ex-US RE	$31,209.95	$37,776.00	$0	$6,566.05	21.04%
Total	$150,739.80	$163,030.00	$523.19	$12,813.39	8.50%

TABLE 8.8. Distribution, dividend and income

Fund	Jan	Feb	Nov	Dec	Total
Vanguard Total Bond		$101.54		$100	$201.54
Schwab US Broad	$80	$74	$80	$87.65	$321.65
Vanguard MSCI Emerging					$0
Vanguard Global ex-US RE					$0
Total					$523.19

Rebalancing

Reviewing a portfolio's performance periodically also provides an opportunity to review its current asset allocation. A portfolio's total market value should come from performance data, and it should be multiplied by each fund's original target percentage to produce individual target values. Individual market values also should come from performance data. Dividing individual market values from a portfolio's total market value will produce individual current allocation weightings. Calculating the difference between a fund's target value and its current value will result in an over- or underweighted position. At this point, you can assess if the weighting deviations surpass your IPS guidelines, and if so, take action accordingly. Dividing the current share price into the value difference will indicate how many units you need to buy or sell. Note: By default, spreadsheet software will use different font colors and signs to indicate positive and negative values. You should have a solid grasp of what needs to be bought and sold before rebalancing.

Transactions

Recording transactions is very useful for tax-related matters and an important part of remaining engaged in portfolio activities. This activity will be of great help to you and potentially your tax advisor. A brokerage may provide a detailed transaction summary in which case your goal would be to review and ensure its accuracy.

TABLE 8.9. Rebalancing tracker

Portfolio Market Value	$163,030						
Fund	Target	Target Value	Current	Current	Difference	Current Price	Shares
Vanguard Total Bond	40%	$65,212	$65,353	40%	-$141	$85	-2
Schwab U.S. Broad	20%	$32,606	$27,400	17%	$5,206	$34	153
Vanguard MSCI Emerging	20%	$32,606	$32,501	20%	$105	$42	3
Vanguard Global ex-U.S. RE	20%	$32,606	$37,776	23%	-$5,170	$52	-99

TABLE 8.10. Transactions tracker

Fund	Date	B/S	Shares	Price	Commission	Net
Vanguard Total Bond	22-Oct-12	Bought	700	$85.00	$9.95	$59,509.95
Schwab U.S. Broad	22-Oct-12	Bought	900	$34.00	$9.95	$30,609.95
Vanguard MSCI Emerging	22-Oct-12	Bought	700	$42.00	$9.95	$29,409.95
Vanguard Global ex-U.S. RE	22-Oct-12	Bought	600	$52.00	$9.95	$31,209.95

DIY Investor: Jennifer Stevens

In step five, Jennifer created a one-page IPS for her IRA account that reflects her overall investor profile, guiding principles, and account objectives. In step six, she constructed her portfolio, selected a broker, and designed her portfolio documents. Before she did anything else, she checked with the fund companies about her investments to see if they were still on a contingent deferred sales load (CDSL) schedule. Of her five mutual funds, one fund is on the CDSL, while the others are free of any redemption charges. Because the fund will incur a penalty of 3 percent, Jennifer will leave the fund as is until it becomes free of penalties. Jennifer also met with her tax specialist to discuss tax consequences regarding her upcoming fund redemptions.

TABLE 8.11. Jennifer's current portfolio

Asset class	Target	Fund	ER%
Fixed income	50%	American Funds Bond	1.40
Equity	10%	Franklin Large Cap Value	1.39
Equity	10%	Fidelity Contrafund	0.81
Equity	15%	American Funds EuroPacific	1.62
Equity	15%	Fidelity Advisor Latin America	2.08
Total	100%		1.43

Source: Morningstar[70]

Jennifer is a balanced investor with a 50/50 split. She has decided to implement a passive investment strategy using ETFs. Her allocation will be 10 percent cash, 40 percent bonds, and 50 percent equities.

- Investment strategy: Passive 100 percent

- Asset allocation: Cash 10 percent, bonds 40 percent, equities 50 percent

Security	%
Mutual funds	
ETFs	100
Individual stocks	
Individual bonds	
Alternatives	

154 / Let's Dance

Jennifer doesn't want to spend a lot of time focusing on financial-market news, but she would like to do more than just pick broad-market funds. While she is an eight-hour investor for her other accounts, she looked at a few investment category funds for her IRA bond and equity allocations. Jennifer decided to spend two hours each week over a three-month period to do research. It didn't take that long to design her new portfolio, but she wanted to consider various options.

TABLE 8.12. Jennifer's new portfolio

Asset class	Target	Fund	ER %
Cash	10%	iShares Barclays T-Bond	0.15
Fixed income	20%	Vanguard Government Bond	0.14
Fixed income	20%	Vanguard Corporate Bond	0.14
Equity	25%	Schwab U.S. Large-Cap ETF	0.05
Equity	10%	iShares MSCI ACWI ex US	0.34
Equity	5%	iShares Emerging Markets	0.49
Equity	10%	Fidelity Contrafund (CDSL)	0.81
Total	100%		0.22

Source: Morningstar[71]

Jennifer evaluated how courteous the customer representatives were at a couple brokers. She discussed her situation and the account opening and transferring process. The customer representative was very helpful, and Jennifer got activities under way. A month later, Jennifer saw that her funds had arrived in her new account. A portion of her account was in cash, while the rest was in kind due to the fund that remained on the CDSL schedule. Jennifer created her documents and calculated how many shares of each fund she needed buy. She went online and made her purchases.

At first, Jennifer was a bit apprehensive about becoming a DIY investor. She thought that she should heed the advice of her advisor and Wall Street professionals, who went through rigorous training to acquire their knowledge and skills. While Jennifer read about investing, it dawned on her that anyone can invest wisely as long as they're committed to learning and exploring other options. Her new portfolio will be managed at a cost of .22 percent compared to the previous 1.43 percent (more when she considers manager trading costs). Based on her investable assets of $200,000, this will be an annual savings of at least $2,420, which she will put toward an annual vacation. Although a couple her previous funds are outperforming the market today, she knows it's only a matter of time before the collective market wisdom bites back. She'll spend less time than she did meeting and communicating with her advisor, so the additional amount saved will come with plenty of upside. By indexing, she's looking to improve her returns because statistics show that many portfolio managers typically underperform the market. She feels empowered and more in control of her financial future.

Eight-Hour Summary

The DIY investor process ends and yet begins with step six: developing an action plan. Timing and fees can have a major impact on investable assets. These two areas bring tax consequences, redemption charges, penalties, and transfers into the mix. Delving into these areas can save you a great deal of frustration in the form of surprises that may inhibit the benefits of DIY investing.

Constructing a portfolio can be a very simple and a fun task. Once you have a handle on your investor profile, type, and preferred investment vehicle, that information will feed into the smaller buckets of investment categories and weightings activities.

Fund companies and brokerages are available to help investors. Through their products and services, they help facilitate the investing process. They also foster economic creation by providing a financial pathway between organizations and investors.

Monitoring and tracking investment activities is the most important ingredient to successful investing. This is where a lot of investors don't pay enough attention. Monitoring performance is how you will make future informed decisions as part of a solid feedback loop.

Becoming a DIY investor isn't an overnight process. It takes time to get familiar with the various moving parts that make for successful investing. It's helpful to set dates and goals as you move from one step to the other. It's also a good idea to consider how important money and time are. You may complete this book and ultimately decide that the cost benefit of using advisors is to your advantage. However, if you can find eight hours a year to manage your own money, the rewards will certainly benefit your lifestyle aspirations more so in the long run.

IX
Oh, Canada!

Maybe Canadians enjoy paying high fund fees.
It's our way of showing the world how good we have it.

As a Canadian, I felt compelled to include a chapter on our investment landscape. For starters, we have a lot to be proud of. Investopedia is one of the largest and most comprehensive websites devoted to financial education. It was started by the Corys—no, not Feldman and Haim, but Cory Janssen and Cory Wagner out of Alberta.[72] ETFs, which have taken the investment world by storm, enable investors to build low-cost portfolios. Canada's financial system is responsible for the ETF model, which was adopted by the United States and the world starting in the early 1990s.[73] And finally, our banks are often rated as the safest in the world, backed by a decent financial regulatory system.[74] Unlike our counterparts in the United States and Europe, our financial systems remained intact and we suffered no failures during the 2008–09 financial crisis. With our accomplishments, one might think that Canadian investors would be ahead of the curve. However, shockingly, our financial literacy is just as poor here, active management performs terribly, and we pay some of the highest fees in the developed world.

A 2012 survey titled the "Canadian Securities Administrators Investor Index"[75] found that 40 percent of Canadians surveyed failed a general investment-knowledge test. You might be thinking the questions were hard, but they were, in fact, fair, and the results regarding some of these questions are very surprising. The survey covered various topics such as fraud, investment knowledge, investor behavior, and market expectations.

Here are a few of the survey categories and their corresponding results:

- **Investment risk:** Sixty-one percent of Canadians understand that stock mutual funds are less risky than a single stock, while 39 percent do not.
- **Diversification:** Sixty-two percent of Canadians understand the concept of minimizing risk by diversifying investments, while 38 percent do not.
- **Mutual funds:** Fifty percent of Canadians understand that returns are not guaranteed.
- **Interest rates:** Twenty-nine percent of Canadians understand how interest rates affect bond prices, while 71 percent do not.
- **Compensation:** Twenty-three percent of Canadians don't know how their financial advisor is being paid, while 77 percent do.
- **Compensation:** Fifty-six percent of Canadians are unaware how much they pay their advisors, while 44 percent are aware.

Financial literacy in Canada needs improvement. When I went to school, courses weren't available to teach students about budgeting, debt, and investing, and only recently have some strides been made. I guess school boards think that gym class and woodworking are of greater importance. Perhaps they are to some, but it's our financial knowledge that will have the greatest impact on our lifestyles and experiences. Investment concepts such as asset allocation and investment strategy found in books are generally transferrable across countries. Therefore, the majority of information in this book is applicable to the Canadian investment landscape. My investment friends in the United Kingdom and Australia also can benefit. Many of them will be seeking a DIY path because banned commissions have changed the investment landscape dramatically. For investors seeking to develop a Canadian literacy ecosystem, I recommend the following resources:

Recommendations

Investopedia is rich in Canadian content and one of the best investment websites dedicated to investor education (heck, we created it). Investopedia is a resource for financial terms, personal finance, articles, and tutorials.

www.investopedia.com @Investopedia

MoneySense is a leading personal finance magazine and website. It covers a wide range of topics, including investing, banking, retirement, insurance, financial planning, education, real estate investing, car buying, and much more.

www.moneysense.ca @MoneySenseMag

Morningstar Canada is a leading provider of independent investment research. Its website provides insightful articles and excellent tools for analyzing securities.

www.morningstar.ca @MorningstarCDN @MstarCDNfr

Globe Investor offers a comprehensive view on investing, personal finance, financial planning, market activity, education, products, and other related topics.

www.theglobeandmail.com @globeinvestor

The Investor Education Fund (IEF) develops and promotes unbiased, independent financial information, programs, and tools to help consumers make better financial and investing decisions.

www.getsmarteraboutmoney.ca @smarter_money

Advisors

As DIY investors or advised clients, it's important to understand the advisory landscape so that a cost-benefit analysis can be performed. Similar to the way it is in the United States, our investment representatives are divided into two groups: mutual-fund representatives (brokers) and investment advisors.

There are approximately 80,000[76] mutual-fund representatives across Canada. They may go by the titles of mutual-fund advisor, investments funds representative, and/or investments funds advisor. Mutual-fund salespeople are licensed to sell and advise on mutual funds only. Similar to becoming licensed to sell mutual funds in the United States, Canadian standards are quite low. The licensing requirement is a course that costs approximately $400 and includes a textbook. The exam consists of one hundred multiple-choice questions and requires a passing grade of 60 percent. Mutual-fund advisors, for the most part, adopt a commission-based model using different types of loads.

Investment advisors (IAs), on the other hand, are licensed to sell stocks, bonds, ETFs, and mutual funds with an option to sell derivatives by taking additional licensing courses. There are close to 30,000[77] investment advisors across Canada. IAs are required to take the Canadian Securities course ($1,000), the Conduct and Practices Handbook course ($650), and the Wealth Management Essentials course ($1,100). Courses and prices can be found at www.csi.ca. The requirements in coursework and cash outlay do a lot to heighten the barrier to entrance. Investment advisors may employ any of the compensations models such as commission-based, fee-based or fee-only.

As reported in the Canadian Securities Administrators Investor Index survey, we know that Canadians are confused about advisor compensation. I wouldn't be surprised if investors were also confused about the two main types of advisors available for advice. There are a couple of easy ways to verify an advisor's status: Ask the advisor what she is licensed to sell or inquire with the provincial securities commission. For example, the Ontario Securities Commission's website provides a search function to check for registered advisors in Ontario. Mutual-fund representatives are associated with the label "Mutual-Fund Dealer," whereas investment advisors are associated with the label "Investment Dealer."

Mutual-fund and investment advisors are salespeople who sell investment advice. Advisors do not have a fiduciary duty to clients; rather, they attempt to fulfill the "know your client" (KYC) obligation to find suitable solutions. The KYC guideline stipulates that advisors should attempt to learn as many pertinent client details before recommending solutions. For example, a mutual-fund advisor is working with a client who has investable assets of $250,000. The client is looking for exposure to Canadian equities, a strategy that is suitable for his investor profile. Because the mutual-fund advisor isn't licensed to sell exchange-traded products such as ETFs, the advisor allocates money to a high-fee Canadian equity mutual fund that satisfies the client's need. Although the client has enough assets to benefit from various investment products, the mutual-fund advisor isn't required to discuss those options. In addition, the conflict of interest between earning an income and providing unbiased advice doesn't affect this advisor, who is seeking the highest possible compensation.

Investment Strategy

Americans are very fortunate to have passive pioneers and advocates of index investing such as John Bogle, Burton Malkiel, and Scott Burns. Canadians haven't been as fortunate to have polarizing voices dictate sound ideologies in their investment community. Their vigor for index investing remains low because the industry is focused on disseminating advisors for salesmanship rather than stewardship. As a result, many investors, by default, adopt actively managed products and services, whether they know it or not. The same logic applies here in Canada—who is anyone to beat the market over an extended period of time? Financial markets are made up of millions of participants and directed by powerful institutional influence. The "chosen" portfolio manager with Buffet-like results is anomalous at best and can be spotted only in hindsight. The S&P Index versus Active report is also available for Canadian investors. Many investors are not aware of it because it isn't in the industry's best interest to talk about it. If investors knew and understood the performance and damaging effects of active "mismanagement," they would flock in droves to index investing.

According to the SPIVA report as of year-end 2011, only 2.74 percent of portfolio managers in the Canadian equity category were able to outperform the S&P/TSX Composites Total Return index over a five-year period.[78] The index is the most watched Canadian index, similar to the S&P 500 in the United States. During the same period, the investment category with the best performance amounted to slightly more than one-fifth of managers outperforming the small/mid-cap equity index. It's obvious that the more plausible investment strategy would be to purchase low-cost index funds. Results highlight the percentage of funds that *outperformed* their benchmarks in Table 9.1.

TABLE 9.1. Active management versus indexes

Fund category	Benchmark	1 Year	3 Years	5 Years
Canadian equity	S&P/TSX total return (TR)	26.67%	8.45%	2.74%
Canadian small/mid-cap equity	S&P/TSX completion TR	31.11%	36.21%	21.82%
Canadian dividend and income equity	S&P/TSX Canadian dividend aristocrats TR	10.00%	0%	9.68%
US equity	S&P 500 TR ($CAN)	8.00%	20.23%	10.99%
International equity	S&P EPAC TR ($CAN)	4.55%	11.54%	6.12%
Global equity	S&P Developed TR ($CAN)	6.56%	11.51%	12.20%

Source: S&P SPIVA Scorecard Year-End 2011[79]

Fees

If Canada falls behind in any one aspect of investing, it's our ridiculously high fees. Our Management Expense Ratio (MER) is the equivalent term to expense ratio. It isn't uncommon to stumble upon advisors selling mutual funds that attract MERs north of 2.50 percent. Morningstar published a report titled "The Global Fund Investor Experience 2011,"[80] which included research on twenty-two developed and emerging financial markets. The company researched various financial system aspects such as regulation, taxation, disclosure, fees, and sales. The total expense ratio, or TER, includes all annual expenses levied by a fund on its investors, covering investment management, administration, servicing, transfer agency, audit, legal, etc. As it relates to fees, Canada was the only country to receive an overall grade of "F." Canada also was the only country with total expense ratios in the highest grouping for each of the three broad categories: money market funds, fixed-income funds, and equity funds.

This point can be illustrated by these three findings:

- Only in Canada and Hong Kong are locally domiciled fixed-income funds more expensive than the asset-weighted median of 1.14 percent.
- Only Canadian and Indian investors pay more than 2 percent for available-for-sale equity funds.
- Only Canada and Italy have available-for-sale money-market funds with typical expense ratios of 0.80 percent or higher.

In a report titled "Mutual Funds Fees around the World,"[81] research was conducted on fees of eighteen countries and 46,580 mutual funds. This academic study, released in 2008, fueled the fire among financial voices here and abroad. The results were in line with Morningstar's report in that Canadians pay the highest fees when compared to other countries, as shown in Table 9.2.

TABLE 9.2. Fees from around the world

Country	Total expense ratio
Netherlands	0.64%
Austria	0.76%
France	0.77%
United States	0.81%
Belgium	0.88%
Ireland	0.99%
Finland	0.99%
Denmark	1.00%
Germany	1.05%
United Kingdom	1.13%
Australia	1.17%
Sweden	1.19%
Luxembourg	1.22%
Italy	1.23%
Spain	1.29%
Switzerland	1.39%
Norway	1.89%
Canada	2.20%

Source: Mutual Fund Fees around the World[82]

Canadian critics could argue that these and similar reports don't make a fair comparison because each country's financial system is unique and thus produces a different TER based on a number of circumstances. However, that's absolutely untrue. Australia shares many similarities with Canada in terms of the number of big banks, investment providers, population, and legal framework, yet the country pays almost half as much in fund expenses. For a developed nation such as Canada, surely our financial system can't be so antiquated that we find ourselves paying more than others globally. In addition, paying hefty fees hasn't produced amazing performance results, as noted in the SPIVA report.

Although Americans pay low fund expenses, we saw the impact fees can have over the long term when comparing passive and active strategies. Despite high actively managed mutual-fund fees, low-cost portfolios can be built in Canada for half a percent or less. So what would be the impact of fees given a TER of 2.20 percent for mutual funds vs. 0.5 percent for a low-cost portfolio of index-mutual or exchange-traded funds? Table 9.3 reveals a difference of $242,000 over a twenty-year period.

TABLE 9.3. The impact of fees

	Passive	Active	Difference
Initial Value	$250,000.00	$250,000.00	
Years of growth	20	20	
Rate of return	7.00%	7.00%	
Expense ratio	0.50%	2.20%	
Net rate of return	6.50%	4.80%	
Total	$880,911.27	$638,507.00	$242,404.27

Under this scenario, the difference over a twenty-year period is almost as much as the initial investment. I would encourage anyone to compute different scenarios because the main point here is to showcase the impact of fees. Canadian DIY investors can build inexpensive portfolios easily. Table 9.4 features a short list of popular Canadian mutual funds, their management expense ratios, and comparable ETFs. These fees don't include additional fees incurred by portfolio turnover and trading costs.

TABLE 9.4. Mutual funds and comparable ETFs

Mutual funds	MER	Exchange-traded funds	MER
RBC Canadian Dividend	1.70%	BMO Canadian Div	.35%
Investors Dividend	2.91%	BMO Canadian Div	.35%
Fidelity True North	2.52%	iShares S&P/TSX 60	.18%
RBC O'Shaughnessy US	1.53%	Vanguard S&P 500	.15%
AGF Emerging Markets	3.07%	Vanguard MSCI Emg	.49%
Templeton International	2.61%	Vanguard MSCI EAFE	.37%
TD Canadian Bond	1.37%	Vanguard CDN Bond	.20%
RBC Bond	1.21%	Vanguard CDN Bond	.20%

Source: Morningstar, BMO, iShares and Vanguard Fund fees and expenses[83]

Fund Companies and Brokerages

The playing field is much smaller in Canada than it is in the United States, but investors have several options regarding fund companies and brokerages. While there generally hasn't been much new development among mutual-fund companies, the growth of exchange-traded funds has helped to expand the list of providers. Although several index-based mutual funds exist, the breadth, depth, and fees aren't impressive. Our five largest banks are Toronto are Dominion Bank (TD), Canadian Imperial Bank of Commerce (CIBC), Royal Bank of Canada (RBC), Bank of Montreal (BMO), and Scotiabank. They all offer index mutual funds. However, TD in particular offers a low cost "e" series group of index funds for investors who have accounts with them. Mutual-fund companies generally do not offer index mutual funds because they focus primarily on attracting assets for actively managed solutions. Exchange-traded funds provide the best opportunity for Canadians to build low-cost index portfolios with expense ratios for some ETFs in the single digits.

TABLE 9.5. Fund providers

Fund company	Mutual funds	ETFs
Blackrock (iShares)		√
Vanguard		√
BMO		√
TD Bank (e-series)	√	

As they do in the United States, Blackrock (iShares) and Vanguard have a Canadian presence. BMO is the only Canadian bank to offer an impressive selection of ETFs.

Brokerages

The five largest Canadian banks all offer discount brokerage platforms. In addition, several more discount brokerages are vying for investors. Commissions vary across the board among financial institutions. The same factors used to consider US brokerages can be applied to Canadian brokers as well. While many brokers are available to choose from, DIY investors should consider Virtual Brokers, Qtrade, Questrade, Scotia iTrade and Disnat (Desjardins Securities).

Accounts

Account types are available for various investment objectives such as everyday investing, retirement, and college savings. The differences regarding accounts typically concern contribution limits and tax guidelines. You should speak to a tax professional about investment accounts to better understand comprehensive tax planning and the impact taxes have on returns. Table 9.6 lists some of the most common Canadian accounts.

TABLE 9.6. Canadian account descriptions

Account	Details
Non-registered	A taxable account that permits individuals to set aside money each year for various objectives
Registered retirement savings plan (RRSP)	A retirement account that permits individuals to set aside money each year, with earnings tax-deferred until withdrawals commence
Defined contribution plan (DC)	A tax-deferred plan established by employers to which eligible employees may make salary-deferral (salary-reduction) contributions on a pre-tax basis

Locked-in retirement account (LIRA) or locked-in retirement savings plan (LRSP)	A tax-deferred plan designed to hold pension funds for a former plan member, former spouse, or common-law partner or for a surviving spouse or partner
Registered retirement income fund (RRIF)	A tax-deferred plan that bridges RRSP assets to pay out a prescribed mandatory minimum payment each year, with no maximum annual withdrawal limit
Life income fund (LIF) or locked-in retirement income fund	The equivalent of a RRIF but for LIRAs and LRSPs with its own withdrawal guidelines
Registered educational savings plan (RESP)	A tax-deferred savings plan designed to encourage saving for future post-secondary costs
Tax-free savings account (TFSA)	A tax-free savings plan that permits individuals to set aside money each year for various objectives

The Day the High-Fee Canadian Mutual Fund Died

The date was September 8, 2006, and Claymore Investments, now iShares, commenced trading of its emerging market's BRIC Index ETF on the Toronto Stock Exchange. For the first time, Canadians could build a complete portfolio of ETFs hedged to Canadian dollars and congruent with their risk profile. This also marked the day the Canadian mutual fund died. Let's first be clear on a few things. Somewhere people are still using typewriters in favor of computers, land lines versus Skype, and video-tape players instead of Blu-ray machines, but the main point is that the former items are no longer mass-produced or current in technology. When the discussion centers on mutual funds and ETFs, mutual funds still have more than $800 billion[84] in assets compared to $50 billion[85] for ETFs, but intelligence will prevail.

ETFs are the smarter, more efficient, more elegant, and more affordable car engine. In Canada, ETFs fall under the same legislation and rules as mutual funds. Their benefits are many, including simplicity, transparency, low fees, tax efficiency, and flexibility. First-generation ETFs, which are those that track market indexes such as the S&P 500, are highly touted for their performance over active management due to their low fees and quality investment strategy. They resided mainly in the hands of institutional investors for years, but DIY investors and forward-thinking investment advisors (mutual-fund advisors are not licensed to sell) are snatching them up.

TABLE 9.7. Canadian ETFs and the year they began trading

Exchange-traded funds	Trading year
iShares 60 TSX	1999
iShares DEX Universe Bond	2000
iShares S&P	2001
iShares EAFE MSCI	2001
Claymore BRIC (now iShares)	2006

Source: iShares[86]

It's worth noting that there were fewer than ten ETFs in 1999, but now there are more than two hundred. ETF net inflows are growing at double digits and outpacing mutual-fund growth. There is now more attention concerning ETFs domestically and internationally. More people are waking up to the impact that fees have on returns, to the dismay of mutual-fund companies. Investors with more than $100,000 in assets sitting in mutual funds should definitely review their portfolio.

TABLE 9.8. Sample MERs for Canadian mutual funds and ETFs

Fund category	Sample mutual-fund MERs per 100K	Sample ETF MERs per 100K	Difference
Canadian Equity	$2,520	$90	-$2,430
US Equity	$3,000	$150	-$2,850
EAFE	$2,920	$370	-$2,550
BRIC	$3,015	$490	-$2,525
Canadian Bond	$1,500	$200	-$1,300

So is the mutual fund really dead? No. In the short term, a mutual fund's usefulness lies with low investable assets and small, regular contributions such as fifty dollars a month. Mutual funds make sense for low assets because of the facilitation of fractional unit purchases, lack of commissions, and convenience. ETFs, passive or active, should be a discussion point when enough assets are accumulated so that buying and rebalancing in round lots, one hundred shares, makes more sense along with their cost benefit. Over the long term, mutual-fund assets and their representatives will falter to second place in the face of more investor-friendly innovations and improved financial literacy.

So where does that leave investors who may be invested in second-rate, actively managed mutual funds? Actively managed funds make a lot of people rich, just not necessarily investors. Their front-running status is fading in the twilight as a once-glamorous product. The date was September 8, 2006, and the logical choice was open to wise investors.

Eight-Hour Summary

Financial literacy is extremely important, but in Canada it's low. We are a developed and educated country with plenty of free resources at our fingertips, yet many of us choose to outsource our financial responsibilities. DIY investing is possible anywhere there is an open and regulated market with the steps outlined in previous chapters. It's really a matter of prioritizing and taking a spirited approach to managing personal finances. The use of advisors shouldn't be the norm; rather, they should be an option for those who have more money than time, are extremely wealthy, or have no time at all. To become an advisor actually takes very little effort compared to the requirements of a lawyer, doctor, actuary, or certified accountant. Successful advisors, those making six and seven figures, are great salespeople. Hopefully those same advisors are successful investment stewards and not the type to dump money into inferior products. If you do hire an advisor, you need to ensure that, along with the correct advisor class, you are enlisting the services of someone who is knowledgeable, practical, and ethical.

Active management is getting outmuscled by a pool of increasingly smart market participants, both locally and abroad. While reasons may exist to use active management, you must question your advisor and yourself to justify your investment selections. In most cases, the fees don't justify the efforts, and if you are unaware of fees, you essentially will be transferring your potential wealth to someone else. The compounding error in judgment will have grave consequences in later years when your dreams and lifestyle choices go unfulfilled. Canadians are getting hammered on fees! With growing interest and solutions though ETFs, our investment landscape is highly conducive to building low-cost portfolios. A slight difference in performance and/or fees has a dramatic impact on returns over the long haul. With additional wealth-erosion factors such as inflation and taxes, investors need to make greater strides in their financial fortitude. For the first time ever, Canadians investors are on equal footing with American investors to make the most of their investing endeavors.

X
Fix You

No wonder retail investors are often left picking up the pieces.

Since the early 2000s, the markets have been a roller-coaster ride wrapped in dishonesty. The dot-com bubble ushered in a plethora of companies with high hopes, short histories, and troubled financials. Who remembers Webvan, eToys.com, or Pets.com? The housing bubble and ensuing financial crisis forced global financial systems to the brink of collapse while the Wall Street upper brass attracted big bonuses and paychecks.[87] Bernie Madoff swindled the wealthiest (who apparently aren't immune to scams) out of billions of dollars, despite Harry Markopolos warning the SEC several years in advance.[88] The bizarre Flash Crash caused the prices of many US-based equities to decline significantly and recover within minutes. Finally, before the Stop Trading on Congressional Knowledge Act, or STOCK, Act was passed into law on April 4, 2012, government officials could freely access and profit from insider trading.[89] Suffice it to say that unreported government insider trading must have transpired for decades while remaining illegal for corporations and citizens. It's amazing how those pesky insider trading details evade campaign speeches.

Now for the goods news…the financial markets are still a wonderful way to create wealth. Warren Buffet, Bill Gates, Peter Lynch, and millions of other people around the world have benefited from financial markets and investing. Market crashes have produced excellent buying opportunities for savvy and patient investors. Product innovations such as ETFs and the proliferation of index funds have made investing more affordable, practical, and simple.

With market cycles, fraud and conflicted advice remain a constant. What can be done to improve the investing process to ensure that all investors are participating on a level playing field? With the research for this book, along with my personal and professional experiences, I have learned that there is a lot that can be done to make the investing world a better place. Expecting securities commissions, government bodies, and self-regulatory organizations to be ahead of the curve is wishful thinking. I would like to support and share a few ideas for Canada, the United States, and financial industries and commissions everywhere. By no means will my suggestions be implemented overnight, but with gumption and a desire to improve the investor experience, a lot more can and should be done. My recommendations are provided in isolation of each other.

Advisor Licensing

Course Fees and Examination Content

Course fees and licensing aptitude requirements need an overhaul. The ratio of knowledge demands to potential earnings is low when compared to other professions, including law, medicine, engineering, and science. It doesn't take much to become an investment representative, and low course fees don't make anyone think twice. At the base level, mutual-fund advisors are typically subject to less stringent content. As a result, the barrier to entrance is low, making the weeding-out process difficult. Ultimately, the examination content, fees, and licensing process should be conducive to attracting client-centric investment stewards and not advisor-centric salespeople.

Recommendation: There could be one comprehensive investment learning stream, with students deciding between two price points—i.e., one to become a broker and one to become an investment advisor. Having a comprehensive securities course will ensure that both brokers and investment advisors have sufficient knowledge outside of their chosen product offerings.

Licensing and Product Disclosure

Advisors should disclose their licensing requirements and product offerings to clients. Many advised clients are unaware of the licensing process. Behind the fancy terms and sales rhetoric lies an easy road. Take an exam here and a few credits there, and presto—you can get licensed to handle people's hard-earned dollars.

Recommendation: Investors should be given advisor profile reports that outline pertinent details about their background and qualifications. This would help reduce fraud and heighten investor confidence. Informing investors about the licensing process is of added value and would help investors with their cost-benefit analysis. As for products, advisors should provide a general overview of stocks, bonds, ETFs, and mutual funds to every client, highlighted by the products they're licensed to sell.

Enabling Brokers to Sell ETFs

Although the mechanics of mutual funds and ETFs are different, the products have plenty in common. Tweaking licensing and regulatory frameworks could enable brokers to sell both types of products.

Recommendation: Brokers should be able to sell ETFs along with mutual funds. This would allow for greater objectivity, fairer dealings, and better product suitability. For example, if a client has investable assets of $250,000, working with a knowledgeable broker may result in an optimal ETF and/or a mutual-fund portfolio solution.

Advisor Responsibilities

Advisors should be left to do one thing: advise. I have found on occasion advisors who double as branch managers. Advisors have access to their own list of clients, but as branch managers they gain administrative oversight to other advisors' clients. This situation presents a potential conflict of interest. For example, a broker with a few high-net-worth clients decides to quit. The broker's branch manager/advisor capitalizes on the situation by assigning those clients to his own responsibility.

Recommendation: Advisors should be disallowed from conducting branch-manager activities. There should be a "Chinese wall" or solid division between advisors and branch managers similar to other efforts made in the investment industry.

Investment Coaching Category

As an investment coach, I want to educate and guide investors to sound investment management. This differs from traditional advice, practices, and services provided by investment representatives.

Recommendation: Create a new investment representation category of investment coaching. Investment coaches would need to complete the same courses and uphold the same standards as investment advisors. They would not be able to hold client assets, nor would they be licensed to sell investment products. Their recommended compensation model would be fee-only without associated dealer, cash grab, or other unnecessary licensing fees.

Advisor Compensation

Ban Commission Model

The Financial Services Authority (FSA) of the United Kingdom and the Australian Securities and Investments Commissions (ASIC) have imposed bans on commission-based compensation. Now it's time for the rest of the world to follow. Commission-based advice is inherently conflicted and acts contrary to the fiduciary duty that advisors should be forced to uphold.

Recommendation: Ban commission compensation schemes and loads paid to advisors. This would promote objective advice, market competitiveness, product fee reductions, and less rogue advisors.

Disclose Compensation Models

It should be mandatory for advisors to discuss all four compensation models (commission-based, fee-based, fee-only, and salary). By outlining the models and discussing their pros and cons, investors would be better positioned to make informed choices. Going a step further, financial institutions and commissions should work together to develop a framework whereby advisors can offer and benefit from all four models.

Recommendation: Disclosure of compensation models should be mandatory.

Disclose Sales Incentives

It should be mandatory for advisors to disclose eligible bonuses for sales targets met. They don't necessarily have to say what those targets are, but they should disclose details about the types of eligible bonuses such as cash, prizes, vacations, and miscellaneous products and services. This would improve trust and transparency between clients and advisors.

Recommendation: Disclosure of eligible bonuses should be mandatory.

Highlight Impact of Fees

The biggest disservice to investors concerns fee transparency. Much more has to be done to highlight the impact and breakdown of expense ratios. An expense ratio should amount to one number that investors can refer to. Investors shouldn't have to search for or calculate hidden fees and/or investment management trading costs.

Recommendation: A portfolio's turnover percentage is of no help to anyone, so the trading expenses portfolio managers rack up should be indicated as part of a total expense ratio. If, during the past year, trading fees amount to .05, they should be added to the current expense ratio with the disclaimer "subject to change."

Marketing & Advertising

Stringent Advertising Compliance

How many times have I come across mutual-fund advertisements highlighting a fund's performance over a one- to three-year period? Countless! A lot of funds marketed their 2009 performance results when markets everywhere experienced dramatic rallies coming out of the 2008 bear market. This was extremely misleading because many funds simply rode the wave. While the industry organizes pat-me-on-the-back award ceremonies for short-term success, only ten or more years of benchmark-beating success is worth acknowledging. Although past performance sometimes isn't indicative of future results, a minimum of ten years demonstrates a consistent track record of decision making and/or luck. Peter Lynch had to prove himself over a thirteen-year period to become a portfolio-managing legend. Others should have to do the same.

Recommendation: Advertised performance results should be limited to funds with activity of ten-plus years. For funds with fewer than ten years of data, mandatory inclusion of inception dates and results should be highlighted.

Side-by-side Benchmark Comparisons

Data on active-management performance is useful only when compared to benchmarks. Many investors are unaware of research tools such as

Morningstar that showcase numerical and pictorial comparisons against benchmarks. Having to view additional websites or take extra steps to aid decision making is antiquated.

Recommendation: All advertisements, fund profiles, fact sheets, and prospectuses highlighting active-management returns should make side-by-side comparisons to benchmarks. Either numerical or pictorial data, or both, should be included.

Returns Net of Fees

Occasionally it's difficult to identify whether results are before or after fees. It's possible that there are official compliance rules regarding this matter, but I've come across a few investment companies that state returns before fees with fine-print disclaimers mentioning that fees have not been subtracted. This misleads investors to select some investments over others.

Recommendation: All returns for public consumption should be stated net of fees. This should be a compliance guideline, if not already, and companies that don't comply should be fined.

Portfolio Manager Scorecard

How about a new revenue card stream for Topps? Or tradable portfolio manager cards? Many portfolio and hedge-fund managers make annual salaries higher than elite professional athletes. Many of these same managers fail to beat the markets year in and year out. Mulling of sporting statistics is a favorite American pastime, so let's introduce statistics on portfolio managers. It's great that they advertise immaterial details such as universities attended, but investors need only one statistic: their track record against the benchmarks similar to the sample in table 10.1.

Recommendation: Portfolio manager bios should include their performance track record against major indexes.

TABLE 10.1. Sample portfolio manager scorecard

Portfolio manager	Jon Stewart
Manager tenure	Since 4/2008
Fund(s) currently managed	XYZ Advisor Strategic Fund
Fund(s) previously managed	XYZ Emerging Markets Fund
Education	BBA, Ohio University, 1993
Historical performance vs. benchmark	4/16 = 25% success rate

Investments

Advisor Portfolio Disclosure

What advice would you get from someone who wasn't trying to sell you something? It's hard to say because it depends on the advisor's character. There are advisors who happily sell high-fee, actively managed mutual funds while their own portfolios hold low-cost ETFs. Conversely, there are advisors who tie their recommendations to their own holdings. Either way, an advised client is subject to *investment-strategy deception*.

Recommendation: Advisors should disclose which investment vehicles they hold. The information would pertain to the broad categories such as stocks, bonds, mutual funds, and ETFs. For example, an advisor recommends to a client a 100 percent allocation to mutual funds. The client reviews the advisor's holdings report of 80 percent mutual funds and 20 percent ETFs and becomes more trusting of the advisor's recommendations.

Active vs. Passive Disclosure

Advisors aren't discussing passive and active management investment strategies. The main reasons for advisors remaining quiet is because they don't understand the difference (the result of inadequate coursework or a poor passing grade) and/or it would negatively impact their compensation (a conflict of interest).

Recommendation: A compliance rule should force advisors to discuss various investment strategies such as passive versus active management. Clients can make informed decisions only when various options are provided. Active-management returns under many scenarios have resulted in clients getting less from their investments.

Asset Allocation Monitoring

I've completed several portfolio assessments. Sometimes the holdings make sense, but other times I'm left shaking my head. While the exact choices remain at the advisor's discretion, and rightfully so, asset classes are less debatable. Equity funds average a higher expense ratio than bond funds, which potentially yield greater advisor payout. As a result, there are compensation-hungry advisors who will allocate to where the money is, despite using common sense regarding investor profiles. The rule of thumb that the fixed-income portion of a portfolio should loosely reflect an investor's age is a good starting point. However, there are advised sixty-year-olds with investor profiles warranting bond holdings, yet they are sitting in 100 percent equity.

Recommendation: Portfolios not containing any fixed-income products and/or bond funds should be flagged for investors over the age of sixty. Secondly, advisors should disclose the reasons for omission.

Pension Fund Stewardship

One of the biggest problems in the investment industry is the lack of stewardship applied to pension funds. Small, medium, and large companies may choose to help their employees save for retirement through 401(k) plans. Companies are subject to the same salesmanship and conflicted advice favoring active management. As a result, many 401(k) plans don't offer low-cost index mutual funds, ETFs, FoFs, or TDFs.

Recommendation: A mandatory requirement of company-sponsored pensions should be to include low-cost, index-based investment options.

Eight-Hour Summary

For the STOCK Act to be addressed only recently is a scary proposition for investors. One would think that some group of officials would have stamped out government insider trading decades ago, but perhaps similar to advisors, they, too, were conflicted. The government and financial industry are far from perfect, but investing isn't perfect. Investors also hold a stake in making the investing process more objective, transparent, and conflict-free. Forward thinking and feedback from market participants to regulators must exceed that of complacency and profits. Only then will many more parties be in a position to have their desires materialize.

Let's not wait for the next financial crisis, the next Bernie Madoff, or SEC oversight to stimulate action. Now is the time to consider which recommendations have been put forth. I provided a few ideas on licensing, compensation, marketing, and investments, but there are many industry faults to overcome. Any facet of market participation provides an opportunity to review the systems in place and ask is this the best that can be done for those involved. If the answer is no, then we've reached an optimal Rubicon. But if we can do more than we should do more because investing is a worthwhile endeavor, the industry should be continually improved for the betterment of investors everywhere.

Eight-Hour Investor

It is your money.
Take care and watch over it.
It is your future!

Your feedback/review would be very much appreciated. Please provide any thoughts or comments at Amazon.com

Follow & visit

www.8hrinvestor.com

www.chadtennant.com

Notes

CHAPTER ONE

1. Tim Maurer, "Mo' Money, Mo' Problems: ESPN Goes," *Forbes*, last updated October 5, 2012, accessed November 15, 2012, http://www.forbes.com/sites/timmaurer/2012/10/05/mo-money-mo-problems-espn-goes-broke/.
2. "Study Regarding Financial Literacy among Investors: Library of Congress Report on Financial Literacy, Part 2," US Securities and Exchange Commission, Federal Research Division, Library of Congress, last updated February 16, 2012, accessed September 7, 2012, http://www.sec.gov/news/studies/2012/917-financial-literacy-study-part2.pdf.
3. "Study Regarding Financial Literacy among Investors: SEC Staff Study Regarding Financial Literacy, Part 1," US Securities and Exchange Commission, last updated August 28, 2012, accessed September 7, 2012, http://www.sec.gov/news/studies/2012/917-financial-literacy-study-part1.pdf.
4. "Study Regarding Financial Literacy among Investors: Library of Congress Report on Financial Literacy, Part 2." US Securities and Exchange Commission, Federal Research Division, Library of Congress, last updated February 16, 2012, accessed September 7, 2012, http://www.sec.gov/news/studies/2012/917-financial-literacy-study-part2.pdf.

CHAPTER TWO

5. "Certified Financial Planner Board of Standards Inc.—History," Certified Financial Planner Board of Standards, Inc. (CFBP), accessed August 10, 2012, http://www.cfp.net/aboutus/history.asp.
6. "Certified Financial Planner Board of Standards Inc.—Around the Globe," Certified Financial Planner Board of Standards, Inc. (CFBP), accessed August 10, 2012, http://www.cfp.net/aboutus/global.asp.
7. "CFA Program History," CFA Institute, accessed August 10, 2012, http://www.cfainstitute.org/cfaprogram/benefits/Pages/cfa_program_history.aspx.

8. "Research & Data," CFA Institute, accessed August 10, 2012, http://www.cfainstitute.org/about/research/Pages/index.aspx.
9. "Why Us—About the College—College Heritage—The American College," The American College of Financial Services, accessed August 10, 2012, http://www.theamericancollege.edu/about-the-college/college-heritage.
10. Ibid.
11. "AICPA Mission and History," AICPA, accessed August 10, 2012, http://www.aicpa.org/ABOUT/MISSIONANDHISTORY/Pages/MissionHistory.aspx.
12. "About the AICPA," AICPA, accessed August 10, 2012, http://www.aicpa.org/About/Pages/About.aspx.

CHAPTER THREE

13. "2012 Investment Company Fact Book," Investment Company Institute, accessed August 17, 2012, http://www.icifactbook.org/fb_ch2.html.
14. "2012 Investment Company Fact Book," Investment Company Institute, accessed August 17, 2012, http://www.icifactbook.org/fb_ch3.html.
15. Norm Champ, "Speech by SEC Staff: What SEC Registration Means for Hedge Fund Advisers," U.S. Securities and Exchange Commission, last updated May 11, 2012, accessed August 17, 2012, http://www.sec.gov/news/speech/2012/spch051112nc.htm.
16. Matthew Goldstein and Steve Rosenbush, "Hedge Fund Fees: The Pressure Builds—BusinessWeek." *Bloomberg BusinessWeek*, last updated May 13, 2007, accessed August 17, 2012, http://www.businessweek.com/stories/2007-05-13/hedge-fund-fees-the-pressure-builds.
17. "Vanguard Target Retirement 2040 Fund," Vanguard, accessed August 17, 2012, http://personal.vanguard.com/us/funds/snapshot?FundId=0696&FundIntExt=INT#hist=tab%3A0.
18. Alan Bjerga, Loder Asjylyn, and Peter Robison, "Amber Waves of Pain," *Bloomberg BusinessWeek*, last modified July 22, 2010, accessed August 17, 2012, http://www.businessweek.com/magazine/content/10_31/b4189050970461.htm.

19. Mark Hulbert, "A Trip Down Memory Lane—MarketWatch," Featured Articles from the MarketWatch, last modified February 12, 2009, accessed August 17, 2012, http://articles.marketwatch.com/2009-02-12/research/30735073_1_e-ratio-stock-market-corporate-earnings.
20. "Shareholder Report," Berkshire Hathaway, Inc., last updated February 25, 2012, accessed August 17, 2012, http://www.berkshirehathaway.com/letters/2011ltr.pdf.
21. "Bogle Financial Markets Research Center," last updated May 2006, accessed August 17, 2012, http://personal.vanguard.com/bogle_site/bogle_bio.html.
22. James Mackintosh, "Hedge Fund Stars Shine above the Crowd," Financial Times, last updated September 11, 2010, accessed August 17, 2012, http://www.ft.com/intl/cms/s/0/981a7710-bcff-11df-954b-00144feab49a.html#axzz2BIc8GmEO.
23. Matthew Schifrin, "Peter Lynch: 10-Bagger Tales," Forbes, last modified February 23, 2009, accessed August 24, 2012, http://www.forbes.com/2009/02/23/lynch-fidelity-magellan-personal-finance_peter_lynch.html.
24. "John Templeton," The Economist, last modified July 17, 2008, accessed August 24, 2012, http://www.economist.com/node/11745591.

CHAPTER FOUR

25. "The Pizza Market in the US: Foodservice and Retail." Yahoo! Finance. Reportlinker.com, October 11, 2012, http://finance.yahoo.com/news/pizza-market-u-foodservice-retail-122300411.html.
26. Christopher B. Philips, David J. Walker, and Francis M. Kinniry, Jr., "Dynamic Correlations: The Implications for Portfolio Construction," The Vanguard Group Inc., last updated February 20, 2012, accessed August 31, 2012, http://www.vanguard.co.uk/documents/adv/literature/dynamic-correlations.pdf?campaignkw=Dynamic-correlations.
27. Ibid.
28. "The Truth about Risk," The Vanguard Group, Inc., last updated January 1, 1995, accessed November 2, 2012, http://personal.vanguard.com/us/insights/investingtruths/investing-truth-about-risk.

29. Ibid.
30. Ibid.
31. Ibid.
32. "Harry M. Markowitz—Autobiography," Nobelprize.org, accessed November 13, 2012, http://www.nobelprize.org/nobel_prizes/economics/laureates/1990/markowitz-autobio.html.

CHAPTER FIVE

33. "Whole Foods Market, Inc." StockCharts, http://stockcharts.com/h-sc/ui.
34. "The Morningstar Equity Style Box," Morningstar Research, Inc., last updated April 26, 2004, accessed September 7, 2012, http://www.morningstar.ca/industry/articles/FactSheetfromUSrenewStyleBox04-26-2004.pdf.
35. "Fixed-Income Style Box Definition," Investopedia, accessed September 7, 2012, http://www.investopedia.com/terms/f/fixed-incomestylebox.asp#axzz21SjNxY7Y.
36. Richard A. Ferri, "How to Find Your Way through the ETF Maze," Forbes, last updated August 26, 2010, accessed September 7, 2012, http://www.forbes.com/2010/08/26/etfs-index-funds-strategy-maps-personal-finance-indexer-ferri.html.
37. "2012 Investment Company Fact Book," ICI, accessed September 6, 2012, http://www.icifactbook.org/fb_ch2.html#assets.
38. Burton G. Malkiel, "How Good Is Fundamental Analysis?" *A Random Walk Down Wall Street: The Time-Tested Strategy for Successful Investing* (New York: Norton, 2011), 182.
39. Burton G. Malkiel, "How Good Is Fundamental Analysis?" *A Random Walk Down Wall Street: The Time-Tested Strategy for Successful Investing* (New York: Norton, 2011), 180.
40. Ibid.
41. Burton G. Malkiel, "How Good Is Fundamental Analysis?" *A Random Walk Down Wall Street: The Time-Tested Strategy for Successful Investing* (New York: Norton, 2011), 181.
42. Lynn Thomasson, "Analysts' Accuracy on US Profits Worst in 16 Years (Update 2)," Bloomberg, last updated August 22, 2008, accessed September

6, 2012, http://www.bloomberg.com/apps/news?pid=newsarchive&sid=akgD2x0SXpPQ.

43. Carole Gould, "Mutual Funds Report—A Seven-Year Lesson in Investing: Expect the Unexpected, and More," *The New York Times*, last updated July 9, 2000, accessed September 7, 2012, http://www.nytimes.com/2000/07/09/business/mutual-funds-report-seven-year-lesson-investing-expect-unexpected-more.html?pagewanted=all&src=pm.

44. Ibid.

45. Emily Wellikoff, "S&P Indices vs. Active Funds Report Scorecard Year-End 2011," S&P Dow Jones Indices LLC, accessed September 7, 2012, http://ca.spindices.com/documents/spiva/spiva-us-yearend2011.pdf.

46. Ibid.

47. Ibid.

48. Ibid.

49. Ibid.

50. Ibid.

51. Charles Stein, "Hedge Funds Lag behind a Generic Stock/Bond Mix," *Businessweek*. last updated July 19, 2012, accessed September 7, 2012, http://www.businessweek.com/articles/2012-07-19/hedge-funds-lag-behind-a-generic-stock-bond-mix.

52. "The Success of Hedge Funds: Masterclass," *The Economist*, last updated July 7, 2012, accessed September 7, 2012, http://www.economist.com/node/21558231.

53. Jonathan Stempel, "Buffett: Index Funds Better for Most Investors," Reuters, last updated May 6, 2007, accessed September 8, 2012, http://www.reuters.com/article/2007/05/07/berkshire-indexfunds-idUSN0628419820070507.

54. Jack Hough, "Time to Follow the Herd," Dow Jones & Company, Inc., last updated August 28, 2012, accessed September 9, 2012, http://www.smartmoney.com/invest/stocks/upside-when-following-the-herd-pays-off-1345842923501/?zone=intromessage.

55. David J. Schwartz, *The Magic of Thinking Big* (New York: Simon & Schuster, 1987), 213.

CHAPTER SIX

56. Anna Prior, "Mutual Fund Trading Costs Go Unreported," *The Wall Street Journal*, last updated March 1, 2012, accessed September 21, 2012, http://online.wsj.com/article/SB10001424052748703382904575059690954870722.html.
57. "2012 Investment Company Fact Book," ICI, accessed September 21, 2012, http://www.icifactbook.org/fb_ch5.html#trends.
58. "Study on Investment Advisers and Broker–Dealers," US Securities and Exchange Commission, last modified January 21, 2011, accessed September 27, 2011, http://www.sec.gov/news/studies/2011/913studyfinal.pdf.
59. Steven G. Blum, "Hiring (or Firing) a Financial Advisor," Forbes.com, last modified July 9, 2009, accessed September 23, 2012, http://www.forbes.com/2009/07/07/investments-standard-regulation-opinions-contributors-financial-advisor.html.
60. Sendhil Mullainathan, Markus Noeth, and Antoinette Schoar, "The Market for Financial Advice: An Audit Study," The National Bureau of Economic Research (NBER), last modified June 30, 2010, accessed on November 1, 2012, http://www.nber.org/papers/w17929.
61. "Financial Advisers' Commission to Be Banned from 2012," BBC News, last modified March 26, 2010, accessed September 19, 2012, http://news.bbc.co.uk/2/hi/business/8589042.stm.
62. Jennifer Hewett, "New Law Banning Commission from Next July Will Change Advisory Game," *The Australian*, last modified October 14, 2011, accessed September 21, 2012, http://www.theaustralian.com.au/business/opinion/new-law-banning-commission-from-next-july-will-change-advisory-game/story-e6frg9px-1226166207447.
63. "FORM N-1A," US Securities and Exchange Commission, last modified February 23, 2010, accessed on September 26, 2012, http://www.sec.gov/about/forms/formn-1a.pdf.
64. "Tax-Deferred Accumulation," Lincoln Financial Group, accessed October 16, 2012, http://www.lfg.com/LincolnPageServer.

65. Molly McCluskey, John Reeves, and Ilan Moscovitz, "Can Your Edward Jones Financial Advisor Really Serve Your Best Interests?" The Motley Fool., last updated December 6, 2012, accessed December 7, 2012, http://www.fool.com/investing/general/2012/12/06/can-your-edward-jones-financial-advisor-really-ser.aspx

CHAPTER SEVEN

66. "FINRA Administered Qualification Examinations," FINRA, accessed October 3, 2012, http://www.finra.org/Industry/Compliance/Registration/QualificationsExams/p011096.
67. Ibid.
68. "2012 Investment Company Fact Book," Investment Company Institute (ICI), accessed October 29, 2012, http://www.icifactbook.org/fb_ch2.html.

CHAPTER EIGHT

69. Fees and expenses, and SEC yield for Vanguard Total Bond Market ETF (BND), Schwab US Broad Market ETF (SCHB), Vanguard MSCI Emerging Markets ETF (VWO), and Vanguard Global ex-US Real Estate ETF (VNQI), Morningstar, accessed November 16, 2012, http://www.morningstar.com/.
70. Fees and expenses for American Funds Bond Fund (BFACX), Franklin Large Cap Value Fund (FLVAX), Fidelity Contrafund (FCNTX), American Funds EuroPacific (AEPCX), and Fidelity Advisor Latin America (FLFCX), Morningstar, http://www.morningstar.com/.
71. Fees and expenses for iShares Barclays Short Treasury Bond Fund (SHV), Vanguard Long-Term Government Bond (VGLT), Vanguard Long-Term Corporate Bond (VCLT), Schwab US Large-Cap ETF (VOO), iShares MSCI ACWI ex US Index Fund (ACWX), and iShares Emerging Markets Dividend Fund (DVYE), Morningstar , http://www.morningstar.com/.

CHAPTER NINE

72. "About Us," Investopedia, accessed October 30, 2012, http://www.investopedia.com/about.aspx#axzz2BerHzjdg.

73. Mark Kennedy, "The History of ETFs," About.com, accessed October 30, 2012, http://etf.about.com/od/etfbasics/a/ETF_History.htm.
74. "Canadian Banks Rated Safest in World," The Canadian Press, last updated April 11, 2012, accessed October 26, 2012, http://www.cbc.ca/news/business/story/2012/04/11/moodys-canada-banks.html.
75. Jason Lockhart, "2012 CSA Investor Index," Canadian Securities Administrators, Innovative Research Group, Inc., last updated October 16, 2012, accessed November 4, 2012, http://www.securities-administrators.ca/uploadedFiles/General/pdfs/2012%20CSA%20Investor%20Index%20-%20Exec%20Summary%20-%20FINAL%20_EN_.pdf.
76. "About the MFDA," Official Website of the Mutual Fund Dealers Association of Canada (MFDA), http://www.mfda.ca/about/aboutMFDA.html.
77. Registration officer from the Investment Industry Regulatory Organization of Canada, e-mail message to author, confirmed number of registrants of 28,902 as of October 10, 2012.
78. Shawn Spencer, "SPIVA Canada Scorecard," S&P Dow Jones Indexes, Standard & Poor's Financial Services LLC, last updated May 5, 2012, accessed July 10, 2012, http://ca.spindices.com/documents/spiva/spiva-canada-year-end-2011.pdf.
79. Ibid.
80. Benjamin N. Alpert and John Rekenthaler, "Global Fund Investor Experience 2011," Morningstar.com, last updated March 2011, accessed September 15, 2012, http://corporate.morningstar.com/us/documents/ResearchPapers/GlobalFundInvestorExperience2011.pdf.
81. Ajay Khorana, Henri Servaes, and Peter Tufano, "Mutual Fund Fees around the World," Oxford University Press, 2008, accessed October 27, 2012, http://faculty.london.edu/hservaes/rfs2009.pdf.
82. Ibid.
83. "Management Expense Ratio," BMO, BlackRock, Morningstar and Vanguard, accessed November 16, 2012, http://www.bmoetf.com, http://www.ishares.ca, http://www.morningstar.ca, https://www.vanguardcanada.ca.
84. "IFIC Home Page," The Investment Funds Institute of Canada, accessed November 15, 2012, http://www.ific.ca/Home/HomePage.aspx.

85. James Langton, "Canada's ETF Assets Top $50 Billion," Investment Executive, last modified August 10, 2012, accessed November 12, 2012, http://www.investmentexecutive.com/-/canada-s-etf-assets-top-50-billion.
86. "Inception Date," BlackRock, accessed November 16, 2012, http://www.ishares.ca.

CHAPTER TEN

87. Michael Corkery, "Executive Pay and the Financial Crisis: A Refresher Course," WSJ Blogs. Dow Jones & Company Inc., last updated September 18, 2009, accessed November 17, 2012, http://blogs.wsj.com/deals/2009/09/18/executive-pay-and-the-financial-crisis-a-refresher-course/.
88. Allan Chernoff, "Madoff Whistleblower Blasts the SEC's Failure." CNNMoney, last updated February 4, 2009, accessed November 17, 2012, http://money.cnn.com/2009/02/04/news/newsmakers/madoff_whistleblower/.
89. "Obama Signs STOCK Act into Law," *Huffington Post Canada*, the Associated Press, last updated April 4, 2012, accessed November 17, 2012, http://www.huffingtonpost.com/2012/04/04/obama-signs-stock-act_n_1402669.html.